M000206648

(Just As Well) It's Not About The Bike

A Journey Across Southern Spain

Chris Atkin

(Just As Well) It's Not About The Bike

First edition. ISBN: 978-1-8384485-1-6

www.chrisatkinonline.com

Table of Contents

Prologue   9

1. Valencia to Gandia   13

2. Gandia to Xàbia   24

3. Xàbia to Altea   31

4. Altea to Benidorm   38

5. Benidorm to Alicante   48

6. Alicante   56

7. Alicante to Torrevieja   60

8. Torrevieja to Murcia   67

9. Murcia   72

10. Murcia to Cartagena   77

11. Cartagena   82

12. Cartagena to Vera   85

13. Vera to Almería   95

14. Almería   105

15. Almería to Beires   108

16. Beires to Guadix   114

17. Guadix to Granada   122

18. Granada   140

19. Granada to Torrox-Costa   150

20. Torrox-Costa   166

21. Torrox-Costa to Malaga   168

22. Malaga   175

23. Malaga to Fuengirola   182

24. Fuengirola to Marbella   191

25. Marbella to Ronda   199

26. Ronda   210

27. Ronda to Alcalá de los Gazules   218

28. Alcalá de los Gazules to Tarifa   228

29. Tarifa to La Línea de la Concepción   236

30. Gibraltar   247

Epilogue   259

About the Author   260

Acknowledgements   261

If you worried about falling off the bike, you'd never get on.

Lance Armstrong

MADRID ●

VALENCIA ○

ALICANTE ○

MURCIA ○

GRANADA

CARTAGENA ○

MALAGA

RONDA ○

ALMERÍA ○

GIBRALTAR ○

0   45   90   135 KM

Prologue

I had long admired the carefree spirit of travellers who bought a mode of transport abroad that they had no intention of bringing back home with them. Be it a car, motorbike or bicycle, they invariably aimed to use it until it collapsed. And if they ran out of road, they were sure of their ability to sell it on afterwards. I'd contemplated adopting the approach myself on a couple of occasions, but my reluctance to pay a relatively large sum up front meant that ultimately I had always shied away from committing to anything more than an airfare.

For several years I'd harboured an ambition to cycle along the Spanish coastline from Valencia to Gibraltar. I already possessed the bike to try. My four-year-old cyclocross Boardman - essentially a sporty hybrid of a mountain bike and a road bike - was up to the task. The thousands of kilometres I'd travelled commuting and exploring the cities, countryside and coastline of southern England on days off had proved that. It had also created an unbreakable bond. One shaped by shared memories of sunny days cycling along rural roads between bright yellow fields of rapeseed and hours spent hunched over the handlebars through driving rain. By recollections of narrowly avoided collisions with reckless drivers, of episodic mechanical failures and of well-deserved ice creams by the sea.

I've cursed my bike hundreds of times, but I've cherished it so many more. My love for it and the freedom it represents is ingrained so deeply within me that it's almost impossible to explain. Non-cyclists may dismiss this as surplus sentimentality. I'll admit that I've looked enviously at friends' sleek, new lightweight road bikes and wondered how much more easily I could climb hills riding them and how much further their wheels would take me. But while my bike looks like a tired workhorse in comparison, its panniers and wider tyres open up possibilities that racing bikes cannot, and the scars it bears tell only the stories of landscapes ridden.

Such romanticism doesn't get around the fact that getting my beloved Boardman to Spain and back would be a hassle. The process of dismantling the bike, packaging it in cardboard boxes for the flight, hoping it wasn't irretrievably broken by an overenthusiastic baggage handler, and then rebuilding it when I landed, filled me with dread. The idea of going through this twice - upon arrival and departure - made me think the free spirits who just buy and sell their transport abroad were onto something.

Obviously, thousands of people travel by air with their bikes every year and only a fraction of them arrive with their frame snapped in two. Everyone told me taking my bike was the logical step, but this otherwise sound rationale failed to take into account another important factor: my poor track record at assembling bikes.

A couple of years before I bought the Boardman, I paid £100 for a new, build-it-yourself bike on eBay. I slowly cobbled it together, but as someone who struggles to construct a spice rack, I had a sense of unease every time I walked past it. My lack of confidence proved well-founded. While cycling 30km/h down a steep hill in south London, my front brake failed and I careered off the road. After dusting myself down, I realised it was because I'd fitted the brake pads the wrong way round. Guilty of such a basic error, the potential for self-inflicted disaster in Spain seemed infinite.

So I opted to buy a bike when I arrived in Valencia. This too failed to go to plan.

I

Valencia to Gandia

I had carefully chosen the bike I planned to buy before I left England, but I wanted to see it in person before entrusting it to carry me 1,300km across Spain. Once satisfied it was the best hybrid bike €200 could buy, I went to purchase it, but was duly informed the model was out of stock and would take a couple of weeks to arrive. Which was far from ideal.

Back to square one, I was shown two similarly priced alternatives that would be available to collect in four days' time. One was a mountain bike, the other a road bike. The latter was ill-equipped for some of the paths I, correctly, anticipated lay ahead, but would be far better than the mountain bike for ascending vertiginous climbs.

Knowing I would need all the help I could get, I pushed worries about punctures to the back of my mind and bought the road bike.

Although I was itching to get going, during my unscheduled delay I learned that Valencia was somewhere I not only wanted to return to, but a place I could see myself living. Spain's third city boasts so many of the things I value: warm weather, beaches, culture, spectacular architecture and a healthy investment in cycle lanes.

Much of my time was spent strolling along the dried up Turia riverbed. The river was rerouted away from the city centre following a catastrophic flood in 1957 that killed 81 people. In some streets the water had been nearly five metres high and in total it destroyed almost 6,000 homes. According to former White House Chief of Staff Rahm Emanuel, 'You never want a serious crisis to go to waste' and after years of being inundated by *inundaciones* (floods), local politicians sensed an opportunity. They sought to build a major new road in place of the river to alleviate traffic congestion. This idea, thankfully, was opposed by residents who campaigned for it to be turned into parkland. Walking along the 9km from one end to the other, it is now difficult to imagine it any other way.

The park carves eastwards through Valencia like a snake heading towards the Mediterranean Sea. It's a popular place for joggers, who run past the sunken riverbed's numerous sports fields, play areas and water fountains. I almost convinced myself that I too might incorporate running into my daily routine if I had this on my doorstep. Close to where the river mouth once was is the City of Arts and Sciences. It's an enormous complex of huge, gleaming white structures hosting an opera house, a science museum, a planetarium and an oceanarium. The ultra-modern domed roofs, glass canopies and angular steel frames dominate their surroundings. The shape of one resembles a giant eye, another a whale skeleton. The buildings are connected via pathways across shallow water, creating the illusion they are floating above their own striking reflections.

Designed in stages around the turn of the Millennium, the site is now almost universally admired, but inevitably, it was deeply controversial at the time of construction. Politicians from the Conservative Popular Party condemned the project as a 'work of the pharaohs' and the city fell into heavy debt as costs spiralled to nearly three times the original budget. Be that as it may, the gamble has overwhelmingly paid off, and the City of Arts and Sciences has been declared one of the 12 treasures of Spain.

Valencia is also home to one of Spain's biggest football teams and attracted widespread UK coverage a few years ago when former England international Gary Neville briefly managed the side during an ill-fated four-month spell. A few months earlier his brother Phil, working at the club as an assistant, had, in an unfortunate misunderstanding of Spanish grammar, tweeted that he had started the day masturbating on the beach. Disappointingly, neither event was referenced during my tour of Valencia's historic stadium, the Mestalla. Our guide glossed over the club's slide into mediocrity over the past decade and focused instead on the glory years at the start of the 21st century, when the team reached successive Champions League finals.

Having collected my bike (a B'TWIN Triban 100 Flat Bar) the previous afternoon, I woke early on the morning of my departure, eager for the challenge ahead. When my possessions had been stuffed into the bike's two rear pannier bags I set off towards Gandia, a town 68km south of Valencia. I began by cycling along the former course of the Turia and across the Assut de l'Or Bridge, its solitary pylon and white cables resembling a harp against the bright blue morning sky. It wasn't yet 8am and the streets were empty as I rode alongside beaches and past the cranes of Europe's fifth busiest container port. Approaching the small suburb of El Saler, I tried to spot a shop to buy breakfast and only narrowly avoided crashing into an oncoming cyclist. I had already struggled to negotiate a roundabout (travelling anti-clockwise around them took several days to feel normal) and the combined 15kg-weight of my belongings which were stored either side of the rear wheel made turning feel precarious.

Both before and during my trip, people asked why I wanted to cycle along the eastern and southern coast of Spain. Apparently the answer wasn't self-evident. I tried to explain the appeal of the open road, the opportunity to not just travel through, but to really be immersed in the environment, and to explore places I would otherwise never get to discover. Sadly, the overwhelming sense of liberation one can feel when riding a bicycle remains unfamiliar to many and I soon realised such an emotive explanation failed to translate.

So I outlined an alternative motivating factor: a desire to improve my Spanish. I had spent the previous five months working as the social media manager at the largest Spanish language school in Panama. Essentially, this involved having a wonderful time and documenting it online to show how great a time you too could have if you studied at the school. In return, I was given tuition and accommodation. By the end of my time there my grammar was relatively sound, yet true fluency continued to elude me. Given the absence of any income, I was also pretty skinny.

I had studied Spanish at school from the age of 11 to 16, but, as everyone knows, language teaching in England doesn't count for much if you want to know anything other than 'where is the library?'. So while this had given me a rudimentary understanding, my Spanish was now a peculiar mix of Castilian and Panamanian. There are thousands of regional differences and I could sympathise with Phil Neville's mistake. For example, in Spain the verb used to catch a bus (*coger*) is the same as to fuck in Latin America. Bus drivers gave me a wide berth, but at least most people seemed to understand me.

Some of my friends had thought I was crazy to go to Panama and believed I was doubling down on this insanity by aspiring to cycle across Spain. I had a wonderful girlfriend, Sarah, who had remained in England while I had been in Latin America. We had been dating for two years when I departed and, after five months away, I'd returned barely long enough to do some washing before I was preparing to set off again to explore new horizons. There is, in truth, never a perfect time to head off alone into the great unknown.

Fortunately, Sarah understood my need to travel and would have joined me in Panama if she hadn't been in the final year of a three-year postgraduate course. After spending so much time apart, we had missed each other immensely and it would have been easy to have shelved my plans to go to Spain. However, opportunity had knocked. I knew it from the moment I received the offer of the job in Panama. I first read the email in a state of shock while sitting on the Docklands Light Railway in east London, en route to one of the final shifts of my expiring freelance contract as a digital producer at BT Sport. Presented with such an obvious sliding doors moment, I intended to jump with both feet. I knew my time in Panama would sharpen my language skills and that on my return to Europe I might never get a better chance to see Spain on two wheels.

Yet inevitably my time on the other side of the Atlantic had intensified my nostalgia for the familiarity of home. As my flight departed for Valencia I was acutely aware of everything I was once again choosing to leave behind. I didn't need to look at my bank balance to know that for it all to be worth it, the trip had to be extraordinary.

***

Just south of El Saler I passed Albufera Natural Park, where a freshwater lagoon is separated from the sea by a narrow strip of pine-forested sand dunes. Not only ecologically significant, the park is also of high cultural importance as the birthplace of paella. The dish was concocted by local farmers and labourers who at lunch would gather whatever ingredients they could find, such as tomatoes, onions, rice, snails, rabbit, and if they were lucky, duck.

When chef Jamie Oliver recently suggested supplementing the dish with chorizo, purists were up in arms. One labelled it 'an insult not only to our gastronomy, but to our culture'. Others sent death threats.

After passing several nondescript villages populated by low-rise apartments, I stopped for a break in a little square in front of a striking cobalt blue building in Mareny de Barraquetes. A man in his sixties soon sat down next to me smoking a cigar. Almost completely bald, his face was lined with deep wrinkles. He wore a stained white shirt, through which I could see the outline of his vest.

Without turning to look at me, he mumbled something indecipherable, before asking, '¿Sabe quien ganó?' Do you know who won?

Racking my brains for last night's football fixtures and beginning to doubt the accuracy of my translation, I recalled the Eurovision Song Contest had been held the night before. He didn't look like your stereotypical fan, but I informed him Israel had come out on top and hoped we hadn't got our wires crossed.

My relief that we hadn't was short lived. The man talked at me for the next 10 minutes, complaining the competition is rigged and that the only country that ever votes for Spain is Portugal. He seemed genuinely angry about the situation. I've always been amazed by the passion evoked by Eurovision. It is the most frivolous occasion imaginable - a European singing contest in which Australia and Israel compete for no apparent reason. I wanted to console the man by reassuring him that, no matter what happened, Spain would at least continue to fare better than the UK. Countries aren't going to vote for the nation that insisted on leaving the European Union. Frankly, it's the least we deserve. We could withdraw from the competition too and save ourselves from the inevitable annual humiliation, but Britons are gluttons for punishment and the chance of us doing so is as remote as the English Channel drying up. Regrettably, I didn't get to share any of this sentiment with my new friend as I couldn't get a word in edgeways. Conceding defeat, I bade him goodbye as he beckoned another man over to carry on the 'conversation'. I could still hear him decrying Turkey's lack of support for Spain as I cycled off down the road.

I travelled through the coastal town of Cullera, where fishing boats and small yachts lined the River Júcar, as I headed south along quiet rural roads. I could feel the sun on my neck as I cycled between fields of lemon trees and olive groves and knew there was nowhere else I would rather be. Apart from the occasional car, the only people I saw were pelotons of lycra-clad men out on their Sunday ride.

I was still revelling in the novelty of the ride when I arrived in Gandia in mid-afternoon. I dropped off my stuff on the outskirts of the city, where I had booked a basic room on Airbnb and met my host Jose and his kind, elderly parents. I then made my way into the centre for one of the most surreal experiences of the entire trip. The population of Gandia swells to more than 200,000 in summer, yet for much of the time I was there I barely saw a soul. To the audible disappointment of my stomach, almost everything was closed. The graffiti that adorned the buildings, the vastly oversized riverbed (filled more by rubble and vegetation than water), and the bolted shutters on the restaurants gave the city an unsettling atmosphere.

In the end I gave up trying to find signs of life and joined a few other bemused tourists in the one place that was open - the ice cream shop. Considering the paucity of customers the woman behind the counter must have had all day, it was remarkable how determined she was to avoid serving anyone. It was as if something terrible had happened in the city and that while everyone else had fled, she had been forced to remain, like the captain of a sinking ship, begrudgingly handing out ice creams to keep up appearances.

Convinced I wasn't missing anything in the centre of town, I walked across the largest of the bridges over the River Serpis in the hope of finding a grassy knoll to lay my head. I had no such luck. What the map had indicated was a park, was in fact scrubland littered with stones and broken glass. I sat on a defaced bench and was soon joined by a wild-eyed, chatty stranger in his forties. We exchanged pleasantries in Spanish for a few minutes.

He then asked me, in the most bizarre cockney accent, 'If you're from London, why don't you speak English?'

I laughed and briefly wondered whether I could convincingly pull off an accent befitting a Guy Ritchie film. I decided it best not to try. He carried on in English, telling me his life story, of how he had grown up in the Netherlands and met a girl while visiting Spain many years ago.

'We travelled across the country and settled in our favourite place we came across,' he said proudly.

'Where was that?' I enquired, hopeful of learning of a well-kept local secret, such as The Beach in Alex Garland's eponymous book.

'Gandia, of course!' he replied cheerfully.

I looked around. He was patently mad. Considering how fond he was of talking, choosing to live in a ghost town was a curious decision.

I returned back over the bridge hoping that, now the time for siestas was over, the city might reawaken. It didn't. Gandia wasn't asleep - it was comatose. I looked for somewhere serving local food to no avail. Forced to admit defeat, and filled with self-loathing, I reluctantly walked into Burger King. Safe to say, this wasn't turning out to be the authentic Spanish adventure I had envisaged.

An explanation for what had, in truth, been an underwhelming way to round off my first day of cycling arrived in a sudden cacophony of sound as I left the restaurant. Hundreds of people were spilling out of the local church as the bells tolled loudly. Embarrassed I hadn't made the connection before, I learned an important lesson: never underestimate the extent to which Spain shuts down on a Sunday.

Obviously, many businesses close on Sundays in the UK and transport services are limited to an extent that one might consider perverse in the 21st century. But Spain takes this to an entirely different level. While cycling across the country I was amazed by the number of ceremonies and festivals in the Catholic calendar marked by Spaniards. The celebration that day was the 101st anniversary of the apparition of the Virgin Mary to three shepherd children in the small Portuguese village of

Fátima. I'd never heard of the reported miracle and thought it odd that the residents of Gandia would honour it with such reverence.

The apparition is said to have revealed three secrets. The first was a vision of hell, while the second is believed by many to have correctly predicted the outbreak of World War II. The Vatican refused to divulge the third. This led to widespread speculation and later became the subject of a hostage demand in 1981, when an Aer Lingus flight was hijacked above London Heathrow. The plane was redirected to France and the passengers subsequently freed following an eight-hour standoff. In 2000 the secret was belatedly published. Many were underwhelmed by it, and some point blank refused to accept its authenticity. This was because the secret didn't contain an apocalyptic prophecy, but 'only' described the death of some members of the clergy. As Cardinal Joseph Ratzinger (the future Pope Benedict XVI) admitted at the time, it 'will probably prove disappointing or surprising after all the speculation'.

2

Gandia to Xàbia

Still unsure quite what to make of the city, I departed Gandia for the relatively short journey to the coastal town of Xàbia. If Gandia's welcome had been insipid, I was delighted by its goodbye: a 7km off-road bike path that took me through fields of orange trees all the way to cute Oliva. An otherwise unremarkable small town, it is elevated by a tree-lined avenue that runs for about a kilometre through the heart of it. I remember it fondly as the place I learned of Mercadona. To Spaniards, this is like saying 'I discovered Tesco', for it's simply a large Spanish supermarket chain, but it came to hold a greater significance. Always a reassuring sight on an empty stomach, it was cheap and cheerful, broad in scope and equipped with a bakery section better than could be expected. I was an instant convert.

Travellers quickly fall into habits to make alien experiences feel a little more normal. My regular trips to Mercadona were just one such example. Each day I would rise early, aiming to be on the move by 8am. In doing so, I hoped to avoid the heat of the day, but invariably, as happened en route to Xàbia, it merely meant I spent more time exploring the places I found along the way.

Depending upon my levels of self-discipline, I would cycle for approximately an hour before stopping to buy some bread and fruit. I always carried nuts and breakfast often consisted of almonds and an orange. Then it would be back on the bike until I stopped to eat a couple of banana sandwiches for lunch. No matter how many times I ate this restrictive diet, if I had stored a muffin, apple tartlet or pecan pastry from Mercadona in my pannier bags, then I felt as though I was eating like a king. Dinner, I promised myself, would be my chance to appreciate the local cuisine - at least as much as my budget would permit. I would not, I vowed, be returning to Burger King.

Two hours later, I arrived in Dénia. I was disappointed to find the town was heavily populated by retired British expats, drawn to the area by its beautiful beaches and year-round sunshine. I'd anticipated this demographic might dilute my Spanish experience and I had hoped I wouldn't come across so many British people until I was further along the coast. I scurried past them, seeking sanctuary in the market hall. It was a hive of activity, with stalls stacked with either fruit, meat or bread. It all looked so good, yet also so similar. The produce varied little in price or quality, making the decision about which stall to buy from seem, to an uninitiated eye, fairly arbitrary. I ate my newly acquired lunch in a small, sheltered park, away from the Brits shouting across the street to one other about what they fancied for dinner.

After lunch I walked up to the town's clifftop fort. Built on top of Roman remains by Muslims in the 11th century, the castle offered impressive views of the town below. The streets were lined with parked cars and the busy, narrow pavements only emphasised the excess bulk carried by some of my fellow countrymen. A large ferry preparing to take people east to Ibiza and Majorca dominated the harbour, while the sun glinted off shiny white yachts in the marina.

What I enjoyed most though was an entertaining dialogue I shared with a seagull looking at me as it stood on the crenellated battlement. No one else was around so I indulged my childish sense of humour and made a seagull-esque 'ka' sound. The bird responded immediately with a 'ka' of its own. We then repeated this pattern for some time as I varied the intervals to satisfy my own scepticism that the timing of my contributions was, in fact, irrelevant. Such worries appeared to be unfounded - my language skills were clearly improving. Smiling, I turned round to see other people had, unbeknownst to me, now arrived at this part of the castle and were looking at me with confused haughtiness. To them I wasn't Dr Dolittle, just another uncouth Brit.

I returned back down to sea level in high spirits. I had stumbled across a town I'd never previously heard of, learned about its history and practised my Spanish in a busy market. This was more like it.

Since leaving Valencia, my journey up to now had been gratifyingly flat and I had somehow convinced myself that, while I stuck to the coast, it would remain so. I was ill-prepared for the challenges that lay ahead having done no training whatsoever for the trip. The furthest I had cycled in the previous year was 25km on a rusty bike in Panama. My naivety is perhaps best demonstrated by my failure, until that afternoon, to connect the appearance of winding roads and switchbacks on the map to the likelihood that a steep hill awaited me.

To plan my route I relied heavily on an app on my phone called Maps.me. Most of the time it was hugely beneficial, but, on occasion, it drove me to despair. In contrast to Google Maps, which predicts a rider's journey time assuming they're Chris Froome, the app gave a much more generous, née realistic, prediction of how long each leg would take to complete and seemed to take into account my need to pause regularly for photographs, food breaks and top-ups of sun cream. If I was feeling energetic, the app's predictions provided the additional satisfaction of having 'beaten the clock' when I arrived at a destination ahead of schedule. Such small victories were sometimes needed after a day in the saddle.

Leaving Dénia, the app suggested it would still take me a couple of hours to get to Xàbia. I found this hard to believe. I'd already made good progress and, seeing my destination was now only 10km away, I gave myself a pre-emptive pat on the back. However, it wasn't long before I realised the error of my ways. While a cursory look at the map suggested I was set to continue cruising parallel to the shore, on the ground I was cycling straight towards the first steep hill of the trip. The Montgó Massif, a vertical rocky outcrop that rises more than 700 metres above sea level, separates Dénia and Xàbia. Luckily, the only road that intersected it required me to climb just one of its smaller foothills, but the unexpected increase in intensity emphasised that I needed to get fit fast.

My calves begged me to stop as I zigzagged my way up the hillside. The drivers of the cars accumulating behind me would have been grateful too, but there was nowhere to catch my breath on the narrow road which was flanked by thick gorse on one side and a precipice on the other. Having slowly dragged myself to the top, I paused only briefly before heading breathlessly straight down the other side into Xàbia.

The town is divided into three separate areas: the pretty old town, situated on a small hill, the port 2km to the east, and the sandy tourist beach 2km south of that. Unfortunately, I failed to find the latter location and wandered, bemused, through the empty streets until I settled on the pebble beach by the port.

Even though it was sunny, the temperature fell significantly in the late afternoon. During those early weeks in mid-May, Spaniards repeatedly told me how unseasonably cold the weather was. I was taken aback, as daily temperatures peaked around 24°C. I love hot weather, but this was more than enough on my rides. So while the Spanish grumbled and held onto their winter coats, I rejoiced. All I needed was for the sea to warm up a little.

As I studied the Maps.me app more closely, I found it calculated the gradient of each route. Forewarned is forearmed. When I looked up the location of that evening's Airbnb, I realised with a sudden sense of dread that in an effort to save money the night before, I'd reserved a bed on the outskirts of town, atop of the hill I had descended only a couple of hours earlier. Reluctant to retrace my steps, after dinner I found an alternative route with countless switchbacks on a hillside covered with half-built houses. The neighbourhood was aptly named Balcon al Mar (Balcony to the Sea) and although my legs were hurting, I undoubtedly had the best view in town as the sun set in the fiery orange sky.

At the summit, I pulled into an empty restaurant car park where I had agreed to meet my host. I hadn't been there long when a battered blue Volvo showed up. The driver window wound down and Beatrisa introduced herself. An attractive woman in her early thirties, she had thick curly brown hair that fell below her shoulders. She instructed me to follow her car until we arrived at the house. I barely had time to nod in acknowledgement before she made a three-point turn and sped off. Desperate not to lose sight of the vehicle, I followed in hot pursuit.

After overcoming the punishing ascent, I was now finishing the day with an unsolicited time trial of unspecified length. By the time we arrived, I was out of breath, my eyes were streaming and I was sweating profusely.

At the property I met Beatrisa's significantly older husband, Eduardo, their five-year-old son and baby daughter. While Beatrisa was extremely welcoming, it was evident Eduardo had misgivings about letting a stranger into their house. This discord was replicated in other Airbnb properties I stayed at. The individual who had not advertised the property would always be civil, but obviously had decided to have as little interaction as possible with guests. Or maybe they just didn't like the look of me. Either way, Eduardo made his excuses and headed out into town. Perhaps sensing his dad's reservations, their son, dressed in his favourite faded blue football pyjamas, growled at me every time I spoke to his mum. Beatrisa and I both laughed as I feigned terror and retreated to the refuge of my room.

Later that night, I was getting ready for bed and walked through the living room towards the bathroom. The dining room table was near the entrance of the room and I was surprised to see Eduardo had returned with two huge pizzas to share with his wife. Rather than walk by in silence, pretending not to see the feast, I instead ventured a 'wow!'. Not my finest Spanish, I'd admit. As I finished the long, exaggerated 'wow', I realised Beatrisa was breastfeeding, making it appear that it wasn't the pizza I was wowing. Mortified, I scuttled into the bathroom and hoped the walls would cave in - something I'm sure Eduardo would have been only too happy to have facilitated.

3

Xàbia to Altea

To my relief, Eduardo was asleep when I got up at 7.30am. The previous evening Beatrisa had recommended that before I descended back to sea level, I first cycled 10 minutes along the road to reach the peninsula of Cape San Antonio. It was the highlight of my time in Xàbia. Time and again in Spain the recommendations of my hosts, which were so often delivered as throwaway comments, led to some of my best experiences. The road from the house cut through an area of dense woodland, populated by pine trees, before opening up to reveal panoramic views of the bay below. I stayed a while, marvelling at my good fortune to have it all to myself. Returning to my bike, I put on my GoPro to record the winding descent I had dragged myself up the night before. Watching the footage back that evening, I felt dizzy.

I soon discovered the Xàbia tourist enclave that I had missed the day before. It was still early, but people were already settling in for a long day at the beach. I was tempted to join them, but knew if I did I'd leave it too late to reach Altea. Recognising my inability to resist temptation, I remained on the promenade which is named in honour of Xàbia's local hero, the famously iron-willed retired tennis player David Ferrer. As I mused at what time of the day it became acceptable to buy an ice cream, I spotted a sexagenarian dancing on the spot as he listened to his headphones with his eyes closed, apparently completely oblivious to the curiosity of the crowd gathering around him. I didn't want to cramp his style by adding to their number, but I too found myself unable to keep my eyes off him. It was oddly compelling to watch.

Wondering what he was listening to, I turned inland and headed south-west to cut off a small corner of the peninsula. A couple of hours of easy riding through the countryside followed before I stopped abruptly, like a horse rearing on the edge of a cliff, when I was confronted by an arresting view. Below me, the sea shimmered invitingly and a colossal, incongruous promontory, not dissimilar to the Rock of Gibraltar, stretched out into the Mediterranean Sea. Three millennia ago the Phoenicians referred to it as the Northern Rock, to distinguish it from its lookalike further south. Close to the rock, a cluster of high-rise buildings formed the resort of Calpe.

Before I could get down to the sea, I had to first

negotiate my way through a maze of holiday homes under construction on the hillside. Each plot was adorned with the branding 'Your dreams begin here' in large font. The fact it was written in English said much about the developer's target market.

My hitherto straightforward journey that morning rapidly turned into a geographical nightmare. The housing development wasn't yet on the map and the ubiquitous marketing billboards made each newly-laid road look the same, causing me to become hopelessly lost. I turned into one cul-de-sac after another as the sea remained tantalisingly out of reach. Having finally found an exit, I stopped briefly at a Mercadona to grab a picnic, before I arrived at the beach and ran straight into the water in my cycling shorts.

Calpe's iconic rock, the Peñón de Ifach, is one of Europe's smallest national parks. The movement of tiny dots at the summit indicated that while I sat eating lunch on the sand, people were walking on the rock 300 metres above me.

I'd have happily spent the rest of the day in Calpe, either flat out on the beach or scrambling up the rock. It was an unabashed, take me as I am, type of tourist resort, happy to trade on its white sand beaches and garish commercialism. After the relative quiet of Gandia and Xàbia, it felt like I had truly arrived on the Costa Blanca.

I chose to avoid the main road out of Calpe and the dark tunnels it cut through the hills. I could see the road from afar and, judging by the weight of traffic and the speed at which the cars accelerated around the bends, this seemed prudent. Instead I set out on a small road used exclusively by homeowners living on a hillside south-west of the town. The route towards the top had so many switchbacks that the GPS on my phone struggled to identify my location, forcing me to guess which street to take. I elicited a mixture of awe and bemusement from residents in their gardens as I edged slowly past them. This bemusement doubled when I descended past them a couple of minutes later, after realising I'd taken a wrong turning.

Eventually I ran out of dead ends to explore. At the peak, the road turned to shingle for 10 metres before terminating at the edge of a cliff. My map suggested there was a path across to the other side of the hill, but I was beginning to learn that it could not always be relied upon. I was hot, tired and frustrated. The view over the Peñón de Ifach far below was impressive, but insufficient reward for my struggles. There seemed no way across and having exerted so much energy to get to this point, I was loath to return to sea level. I walked around until I found a dusty path in the right direction that was tucked away between two houses and marked by a no entry sign. Undeterred, I hastily hopped over the low metal chain.

Relief washed over me when I found the connecting road down the other side. My lung-busting efforts hadn't been in vain and I looked forward to a relaxed ride back to sea level, followed by a gentle meander along the coastline towards Altea. The road, though, had other ideas. Close to the start of the descent was by far the steepest road I'd ever ridden. I began by getting on my bike alongside two partially constructed houses which looked like they had been untouched for some time. I suspected the builders had got fed up walking up to the site, or that their vehicles had given up en route. To avoid going straight over the handlebars, I leant back to put as much downforce as possible on my rear wheel. The weight of my pannier bags, which had been such a millstone on the way up, was now a virtue.

I subsequently calculated the gradient of this stretch of road and learned it was 22% - making it one of the steepest in the country. To put this in perspective, even the most imposing mountain stages of the Tour de France aren't as ridiculous as this. The Alp d'Huez is one of the race's most iconic, and painstaking, climbs, yet even here, the maximum gradient of the mountain roads is 'only' 12%. It doesn't matter how heroically fit or pharmaceutically assisted you are, some roads are not meant to be conquered in the saddle. I descended comically slowly, tentatively releasing the brakes a fraction of a second at a time, as I inched my way down the slope.

Following a few wrong turns, I returned to the shore considerably more drained than I had been when I set out from Calpe. The journey would have taken less than 15 minutes by car and, if a passenger in the vehicle had even registered the route they had taken, they would almost certainly soon have forgotten it. While the metal box of a car cocoons its inhabitants, a bike exposes a cyclist to the environment. It is both a blessing and a curse. Back by the sea, I cycled along an off-road coastal bike path, next to small upturned fishing boats laid out in preparation for the morning, and listened to the water gently lapping onto the beach.

It was never easy predicting for my hosts the time I would arrive at my destination each evening. To give myself plenty of leeway, I always greatly overestimated the journey times. When I was lost in the hills above Calpe, this was at least one decision I was pleased to have made. So as I arrived at the bleach white pebble seashore of Altea in the last rays of the evening sun, I still had time to find dinner before going to my accommodation. I entered a restaurant on the seafront and enquired about their advertised soup of the day.

'*Es sopa de mariscos,*' the owner told me. It's seafood soup.

He walked me over to a table and added quietly, '*Siempre es sopa de mariscos. Si lo cambio, los lugareños se molestan mucho.*' It's always seafood soup. If I change it, the locals get very upset.

I laughed, assuming he was joking, but his expression said otherwise. My scepticism was swept away when the soup was served. It was delicious.

Upon arriving at my accommodation I was met by a tall, angular woman in her mid-forties named Anne.

'*¡Buenas tardes! ¿Cómo está?*' I said cheerfully. I was always keen to speak in Spanish with my hosts and corresponded via texts in the language prior to meeting them. Despite the effort I put into my carefully crafted messages, or perhaps because of the errors they contained, Anne refused to countenance the idea of using Spanish face-to-face.

'Hello,' she responded in a friendly, if slightly guarded tone.

'*¿Podemos hablar en Español?*' I asked hopefully. I owed it to myself to at least try to speak Spanish whenever I could.

'No, let's speak in English,' Anne said with finality. 'I'm not Spanish and neither are you.'

I couldn't argue with her logic and I could tell any attempt to do so would be futile. Her directness led me to guess she was German, but she was in fact Dutch. Nonetheless, her Spanish would almost certainly have been flawless, having lived on the Costa Blanca for more than 20 years.

Anne showed me to my room. Like the vast majority of the places I stayed, it was small and plain, adorned with a single bed, a desk and a cupboard, the latter two of which I knew I wouldn't use.

'Would you like another pillow?' she asked.

I looked at the two pillows already on the bed. 'These will be fine thanks,' I replied, knowing I could sleep practically anywhere after a day on the bike.

'I'll get you another,' she insisted.

She reached to the top of the cupboard and brought out one pillow after another of varying sizes, weight and compactness. It was soon difficult to see the floor underneath. Either Anne had previously hosted some remarkably fussy guests, or she was worried about an impending national pillow shortage. I chose one at random and we returned to the kitchen.

Anne lived alone and was eager to chat. She began by criticising Airbnb's admin fees before moving on to discuss broader topics such as the problem with social media, the internet and Generation Z. I had hoped to plan my route for the following day, but when I at last managed to excuse myself a few hours later, I could do little more than crawl into bed.

4

Altea to Benidorm

In the morning, Anne suggested I visit Altea's old town as she handed me a slice of toast. I had just taken my first bite when she said matter of factly, 'I'm pleased you're nice...I ended up strangling the last guest who came to stay.'

I wasn't sure how to react. Was this day to be my last? I hoped I hadn't chosen the wrong pillow. I tried to read humour into her expression, but it was clear she wasn't joking, so I tried to make it look like I didn't think strangling guests was a big deal.

Unable to hold herself back any longer, Anne launched into a 20-minute diatribe describing the tensions surrounding a long-term guest who had refused to leave. It seemed inappropriate to eat my toast like popcorn at a cinema while she recounted her tale and it soon went cold and brittle in my hands.

'After weeks of trying to put up with her, I couldn't take it anymore. I wanted her out of my house and out of my life. When she screamed at me in the hallway, I pushed her against the wall and held her there by the throat. She tried to struggle free, but she was a small Chinese girl so it made little difference.'

An image floated into my mind of a cartoon character holding up another by the throat so that the victim's feet hung helplessly in the air. I bit my lip to stifle an ill-timed smile.

'When I let her go, she ran out the door and the next day arranged for someone to pick up her things. I never saw her again. I know what I did was wrong, but it was like psychological torture living with her.' Anne finally paused. 'Do you understand?'

I could see how much she wanted me to condone her behaviour. Unfortunately, I was still lost for words. I exhaled audibly, before adding diplomatically but unconvincingly, 'Yeah...some people are odd, I guess.'

Eager to avoid learning of any more skeletons in Anne's closet, I set out to explore Altea on foot. The old town was on a hill set back from the coast so if it wasn't for the recommendation I may well have missed it. I'm glad I didn't. Of all the quintessentially Mediterranean towns I cycled through, Altea was quite probably the prettiest. The contrasting colours of the whitewashed houses, the terracotta roofs, the verdant violet flowers and the views overlooking the deep blue sea made every street look like it belonged on a postcard.

Looking back towards where I had cycled from the

day before, I could see the unmistakable shape of Peñón de Ifach still dominating the skyline. The Parc Natural de la Sierra Helada, literally translated as the natural park of the ice mountain, lay to the south. Mercifully, I would be circumventing the mountain itself by heading south-west, where 10km away, I could see the outskirts of a place that couldn't be more different from Altea's tranquil, understated beauty: Benidorm.

The previous evening I had told Anne it was to be my next stop.

'But why would you want to go there?' she asked in a mixture of confusion and genuine horror.

'I've heard so much about it,' I replied. 'And as it's so close, I'm intrigued to see what it's like.'

It was reminiscent of the scene in *The Lion King*, where Mufasa tells his young son the Shadowlands is the place he 'must never go'. But just as Simba is drawn to the darkness in spite of all the sunny uplands around him, I too couldn't resist exploring a destination the mere mention of which evokes arched eyebrows.

I carried on wandering through the narrow cobbled streets of the old town and around the blue-domed church of The Virgin of the Consol. I wanted to get my fill of culture as I suspected it would be in short supply in Benidorm. When I first conceived the idea for this trip, I intended to come upon a town I liked that wasn't too big or too English and find a job in a bar or cafe so I could support myself for a few months while I sharpened my Spanish. The plan never came to pass. Sarah was now set to finish her course ahead of schedule in order to start a new job beginning in July. In the circumstances, extending our time apart beyond the seven months I had already instigated would have been gratuitous. Nevertheless, as I headed back to Anne's house to collect my bags, I reflected that Altea was the kind of place that would have fitted the bill almost perfectly.

The Iberians, Greeks, Phoenicians, Romans and Muslims were similarly charmed by Altea and all left their imprints on the town. More recently, in the 1960s and 1970s, the town attracted a bohemian crowd of famous individuals. Rafael Alberti, regarded as one of Spain's greatest literary figures and recipient of the Lenin Peace Prize, was one such resident. Singer and actress Pepa 'Marisol' Flores was another. A superstar from the age of 11, she had powerful supporters including the country's military dictator, General Francisco Franco. He was an avowed fan who believed the singer's performances captured a buoyant mood that could, and should, sweep the country. Although she benefitted immeasurably from Franco's endorsement, Marisol was a lifelong socialist and privately despised everything he stood for. She is reported to have put all the awards Franco gave her up for auction, with the proceeds donated to Spain's Communist Party. In 1982 Marisol went even further. She travelled to Cuba to marry and named the revolutionary leader Fidel Castro to be her children's godfather.

But I digress. Due to the delay picking up my bike in Valencia, time wasn't on my side to explore more of Altea. After wishing Anne better luck with future guests, I hit the road and headed to Benidorm. Did it live up to its billing? You better believe it.

A one-time tiny fishing village that can trace its existence back to 1325, Benidorm changed beyond all recognition during the second half of the 20th Century. The town developed into a city and at one stage received one in every 10 visitors to the country. While Benidorm's golden years may now be behind it, it remains Europe's biggest holiday resort, attracting five million tourists every year. The groundwork for all of these achievements was laid by an enterprising man named Pedro Zaragoza.

Zaragoza was born into a poor family of sailors in Benidorm. As a young adult, he struggled to make ends meet, working at various stages as a travelling salesman, a miner and a porter at a train station in Madrid, before returning to his hometown as a bank manager following the death of his father. Back in Benidorm, he caught the eye of government officials, who appointed Zaragoza as the town's mayor in 1950. He was just 28 years old. At this stage, Benidorm had a dwindling fishing industry and only 102 hotel rooms. The young mayor had plans for something greater.

Using all the flair he had accrued as a salesman, he travelled across Europe encouraging everyone to visit Benidorm. He raised the little town's profile by using unorthodox methods such as planting orange trees, naming them in honour of famous people such as Queen Elizabeth and Charles de Gaulle, and sending the fruits directly to their namesakes.

As visitors from Britain and northern Europe began to arrive, they brought with them an item they considered unremarkable, but was outlawed in Spain: the bikini. In 1953 Zaragoza announced they would be allowed in the town. This represented a huge personal gamble as his proclamation directly contradicted Franco's ban. No one else in the country had attempted such a bold move and the stunt could well have seen him removed from office. Predictably, in a Catholic country under heavy censorship, Zaragoza's stance created uproar. Members of the Civil Guard scuffled with scantily-clad girls on Benidorm's beaches and local archbishops threatened to excommunicate the mayor. Yet he saw no problem with the bikinis and believed Franco's law would be impossible to police as the number of tourists travelling to Spain increased. So he set off at 6am one morning on his Vespa to appeal directly to Franco. According to *The Economist*, when Zaragoza arrived in Madrid eight hours later, 'the dictator, amused by this small, round, moustachioed man with motor oil on his trousers, became a fan at once'. Bikinis were permitted to remain in Benidorm.

Although the archbishops dropped their threats, members of the clergy continued to be obdurate. In 1960 the bishop of nearby Orihuela threatened to place signs by the road into Benidorm, informing visitors that the mayor and the town's residents would go to hell for accepting bikinis, or as he memorably described them, 'garments of sin'. Just like the promise of excommunication, this threat too was later dropped. (These bishops are all talk.) Local Catholic monks did belatedly make a stand two years afterwards when they installed a cross on top of the Sierra Helada. For them it was the culmination of a mission to prove that Benidorm had not lost its soul by opening its arms to bikini-wearing tourists. One can only imagine how they felt when visitors began sunbathing topless.

For a man whose leadership saw this tiny village change beyond all recognition, you would expect to find a range of opinions regarding the policies he implemented during his time in office between 1950 and 1967. However, as long as you don't ask the monks, public sentiment is still overwhelmingly positive about his legacy. When he died in 2008, the town observed two days of mourning. One of the reasons Zaragoza is still revered is because he had the foresight to insist all new hotels were designed as high-rise buildings. This preserved space for parkland and enabled people to see the beaches and feel the sea air. The city's council continued to implement the policy after he retired, so by the time of his death, Benidorm was home to 330 skyscrapers - the highest number of high-rise buildings per capita in the world.

While Zaragoza's vision for Benidorm was unquestionably successful, the reputation that precedes the city today is not entirely undeserved. At times it feels like teams at the European bingo championships have chosen to leave the stuffy community halls behind for a trip in the sun. Minus their clothes. Benidorm's tourist board may market itself as a party town, but it would appear the sheer number of wrinkly naked breasts has scared off young partygoers, leaving the old to dominate.

In 2010 there was a wonderfully bizarre, and extremely popular, Flemish television series called *Benidorm Bastards*. The series, which can still be found on YouTube, featured elderly actors behaving badly in Benidorm. They were filmed swearing loudly, selling drugs and generally doing anything they could to shock the young. The show's popularity was such that it spawned similar series in 12 other countries, from Estonia to the US. Benidorm's mayor at the time was not amused and threatened legal proceedings, demanding that the show be renamed. He was not affronted by the vulgarity and had no issue with the term *Bastards*, but he insisted the mention of *Benidorm* had to go. His wishes were ignored.

You can say what you like about the city, but it still draws the punters. It was the busiest - and worst - seaside location of the trip so far. Watching people jostle through the crowds outside trashy restaurants, bars, clubs and shops, I couldn't help but wonder whether some of the visitors would have been happier in Altea. It was so near, yet to the uninformed and sedentary holidaymakers, so far. They would never know what they had missed. And for that, residents of Altea such as Anne, were grateful.

I passed a waterfront bar offering £1 pints that had *Twisting by the Pool* by Dire Straits blaring out of the sound system. It epitomised much of Benidorm. The city's establishments know what people want and understand that they appreciate the familiarity of a place they come back to year after year. So why change? It's far easier to keep everything as it was in 1983.

Just when I was ready to dismiss Benidorm as the vacuous, hedonistic resort I had been warned about, it actually began to grow on me. While it is easy for outsiders to be po-faced about the tacky bars and nightclubs, there is something admirable about a place that's unconcerned about being cool or cutting edge, and is unashamedly set up for people to enjoy themselves. Moreover, for a city that doesn't attract many cyclists, it has an unexpectedly well-developed network of bike lanes. Again, some of the credit for this can be attributed to Pedro Zaragoza. He oversaw the construction of wide roads, confident that while they were grossly oversized when they were built, they would be needed when his vision became reality. As any town planner knows, it is a lot easier to add cycle lanes when a city isn't already clogged with narrow one-way streets.

Benidorm has two main long arcing bays named Playa de Levante and Playa de Poniente. This means that wherever you sunbathe, you can forget about at least half of the city's tourists. I hadn't expected it, but with the exception of the odd cigarette butt, the beaches were pristine. Midway through the afternoon, I hauled myself off the sand to find my accommodation. My map initially led me to a property at completely the opposite side of town to where I should have been, so after clocking up some unexpected kilometres, I eventually met my hosts.

Ben and Phil were a friendly gay British couple working as chefs in the kitchens of two local restaurants. After my failure to speak Spanish with Anne, I didn't even try to convince them to eschew English. Instead, I listened to their plans for what promised to be a big weekend ahead. They were looking forward, yet evidently also slightly dreading, attending a colleague's marriage ceremony. Ben confidently asserted that despite the fierce competition, the event would be 'Benidorm's queer wedding of the summer' and they intended to carry on the celebrations through to the following day for the Royal nuptials of Prince Harry and Meghan Markle.

I returned to the city centre and visited the headland that separates the two largest beaches. Illustriously named the Balcón del Mediterráneo, it has surprisingly tasteful white palisades that lead down to a tiled veranda of the same colour. It was blinding to look at and heaving with tourists who had gathered to watch the sunset. I spent some time admiring the unparalleled views over both bays before I turned back towards the sound of Bryan Adams' *Summer of 69*, which was pumping obnoxiously somewhere on the shoreline. Feeling hungry, I did what any self-respecting British tourist would do in Benidorm. I ignored the overpriced and inauthentic tapas restaurants and ate fish and chips for dinner on the beach. Later, I watched the Europa League final at a local bar. The customers were almost all Spanish and they went home happy after seeing Atletico Madrid defeat Marseille.

5

Benidorm to Alicante

I could happily have stayed longer in Benidorm, but having anticipated being left cold by the city, I had already booked the next night's accommodation in Alicante. So I left behind the shiny, neon metropolis and travelled inland, arriving after a couple of hours at the deserted Amadorio Reservoir. The milky turquoise water looked enticing, but much of it was enclosed by a dusty open-pit mine, the vast emptiness of which gave the site an unsettling atmosphere. It was the kind of place you'd go to dispose of a body and my self-imposed isolation, which I usually found so liberating, suddenly felt oppressive.

I relieved the tension by playing Spanish songs on my phone. No one, I reasoned, dies listening to Enrique

Iglesias. The distraction successfully eased my disquiet, but the stifling temperature could not be so easily drowned out. I learned it was one thing to cycle in the middle of the day aided by a cooling sea breeze, but quite another to do it in a sweltering mine devoid of shade. As the route ascended the road surface deteriorated into shingle. The hills were not steep kilometre-long climbs - those were to come later in the trip - but rather a series of unrelenting small inclines. It was impossible to see what was beyond the brow of each hill, allowing me to foolishly hold out hope that I was always just about to arrive at the summit. As the last of my energy drained from my legs, the terrain finally plateaued. Soon I was riding on tarmac again and I popped out at a T-junction as two neighbours chatted outside the first houses I had seen for several kilometres. They looked as astonished to see me as I was to see them. When they asked me where I was going they laughed good-naturedly at my response and pointed me downhill towards the coast.

I hadn't travelled far when I reached Aigues seeking food and water. To my disappointment almost everything was closed, but it was charming all the same. In many ways Aigues was the perfect example of a rural Spanish village. Its pretty little square was demarcated by raised flowerbeds. At one end was the entrance to the church, the building's humble design juxtaposed with remarkable harmony by the addition, on one of the bell towers, of a large white clock with black Roman numerals. At the other end was the very welcome sight of a water fountain.

Aigues' location more than 300 metres above the Mediterranean shore, and 20 minutes' drive from the nearest town, has served to insulate it from the impact of the rising number of visitors to the Costa Blanca. The only people I saw were a few old men with mahogany coloured skin silently smoking pipes as they watched the world go by. It struck me as a pleasant, if unrewarding, way to spend time, given that my appearance was probably one of the few variations between that day and any other.

I continued towards the town of El Campello, freewheeling down the quiet roads almost all the way to the sea. Having sated my thirst, I sought out the nearest bakery like a heat-seeking missile and bought a couple of palm-sized pizzas and small pastries fresh out of the oven. I devoured them on the neighbouring beach. A fierce sea breeze swirled around me and the softness of the dough was thrown into sharp relief by the grittiness of the grains of sand that inevitably entered my mouth. It was a price willingly paid for the setting.

A stubby cylindrical stone tower, built in the 16th century to forewarn residents about the presence of pirates, stood by the harbour at the northern end of the promenade. Its formidable walls gave it the appearance of a castle bastion and the only entrance was a small door located five metres above the ground.

Further along the coast, the 4km-long esplanade lined with palm trees, restaurants and shops was empty. So too was the immaculate beach; evidence that although the temperatures were rising, the main tourist season was yet to begin. I had the place to myself, but unlike in the open-pit mine of the Amadorio Reservoir, I felt on top of the world. The holidaymakers battling for space to lay their towels in Benidorm were unaware an entire coastline was theirs for the taking only half an hour's drive away.

Benidorm's regional dominance puts the scale of Pedro Zaragoza's achievement into context. Back in the 1950s, his seaside village was just one of several that could have been transformed into an international tourist hot spot. Yet his efforts ensured it was Benidorm that was the name on everyone's lips.

When I reached the end of the beach I turned west towards Alicante. The city's urban sprawl has been partially thwarted to the east by the vertiginous Sierra Grossa, a 161m-high peak close to the waterfront. Used as a viewpoint since the Bronze Age, the area is now the preserve of hikers looking for a place to stretch their legs away from the beach. I was looking for quite the opposite, so I carried on negotiating my way through the city's confusing web of cycle lanes and one-way streets.

I arrived at the marina, replete with its array of eye-catching superyachts and locked my bike. Before beginning my journey across Spain, I had been shocked to learn many cyclists don't carry a bike lock with them on long-distance road trips. Such purists regard locks an unnecessary burden, advocating that a rider should never be far from their bike during the day, should bring it indoors at night and learn to trust in the innate goodwill of others. My lock was undeniably heavy and I would have dearly loved to have gone without it. However, I've had a bike stolen before and I'm the kind of person whose bike you can find at home locked to a fixed point in a locked shed in a locked garden. Sadly, even the free spirit within me needs reassurance I will find my bike where I left it.

After fastening my bike to a post, I removed from my pannier bags a rucksack containing only valuable or useful essentials (sun cream, wallet, passport, nuts, travel towel and a bottle of water) and went off to explore the city. This unpacking process, painfully slow when I left Valencia, had quickly been refined by practise and now took no time at all. Unlike the bike itself, I rarely worried any misfortune would befall the possessions I left behind. Anyone rifling through them would have found only a pair of flip flops, a pair of swimming trunks, some smelly T-shirts, socks and underwear and an emergency purchase of a hideous, swampy green jumper I had bought in Benidorm to counter the unexpected chill of the evening air. Knowing many of the items would be unlikely to survive the journey, I had brought some of my worst clothes with me, and as my friends would attest, there was no danger anyone would want those.

Running parallel to the marina was the famous Explanada de España. One of Spain's most famous esplanades, this is the place to be seen in Alicante. Well-dressed couples walked along the white, black and orange tiles of the shaded avenue as artisans competed for custom. Covered as I was in sweat and sand, I felt distinctly underdressed in my salt-marked T-shirt and politely declined the opportunity to have my portrait drawn.

Besides, I had a greater prize in mind: an ice cream on the beach. Unsurprisingly given its central location, the popularity of El Postiguet Beach was in stark contrast to the shore at El Campello. I spent the rest of the afternoon on the sand before heading across the city to meet my Airbnb host Esteban. Or maybe it was Mauro. He had written both names down on different parts of his online profile, meaning I was unsure how to greet him in person. I never found out, so let's call him Steve. Greeting me at the door, he barely said a word and my efforts to make conversation as we ascended the four flights of stairs received only monosyllabic responses. Four floors is a long way to walk in almost complete silence with a total stranger.

Upon arriving at the door to his flat, Steve showed me to my room, pointed to the keys and wifi password on the table and promptly turned on his heels. As I unpacked, I reflected on the variety of Airbnb hosts I had stayed with over the past few days. Some individuals such as Anne were eager to meet new people and exchange stories, while others, such as Steve, used the site purely as an additional revenue stream. I never knew what to expect each time I knocked on a host's door, but I learned not to take occasionally brusque behaviour to heart.

From my room I overheard a female voice with an English accent speaking excitedly to Steve in the kitchen. She was discussing the growth of his magic mushrooms and at what point they would be ready to be sold. It seemed Steve was quite the entrepreneur. He quickly left what had been a very one-sided conversation, and as I walked towards the front door I stuck my head into the kitchen to introduce myself. The voice had come from Steve's flatmate, a 23-year-old who had grown up in Walthamstow in north-east London. She was as high as a kite. I barely got a word in edgeways as she told me about her move to Spain nine months ago, her life in Alicante and her few brief attempts at learning the language. After

15 minutes I guessed why Steve avoided conversations with English people.

By the time I escaped the flat it was dark, so I ate dinner at a popular tapas restaurant nearby. I have mixed feelings about tapas. Obviously, it's tasty, fun and steeped in cultural heritage. The restaurants are fascinating places to watch locals interact and I enjoyed practising my Spanish while eavesdropping on snippets of their conversation. However, from the budget cyclist's perspective, tapas has its limitations. At the end of a day spent burning calories, a slither of fish, meat or cheese on top of two bites of bread simply doesn't cut it.

A selection of four types of tapas comes to more than €10, but still feels like what it is; a snack. Moreover, if you're not buying a *ración* (a main course), many restaurants will prohibit you from sitting at a table and insist you eat at the bar. While this provides an excellent vantage point to watch the perpetual motion of organised chaos all around, there's little opportunity to relax because once you have chosen your tapas, it is served almost immediately, with the bill issued right away and the plates cleared as soon as you've finished. It's understandable that restaurant owners want a healthy turnover of customers, but when your budget is stretched and you just want to sit down on a seat unconnected to pedals, it's preferable not to have to choose between walking to another bar for a drink or going to bed 20 minutes after picking up a menu.

Having failed to find a bar close by, I wandered back towards Steve's flat. During my trip, I was reluctant to reserve any accommodation on Airbnb for more than one night at a time, in case my host had a penchant for strangling guests. As the first major city on my route since I left Valencia, I had much more to see in Alicante and intended to make the next day my first rest day. In spite of my reservations about Steve, I would have booked to stay another night, but it seemed he was a man in demand and the room was no longer available. Or perhaps he just wanted rid of me. Either way, there weren't any suitable budget options on Airbnb at such short notice so I began searching online for some hostels to try the following morning.

6

Alicante

Alicante's most iconic monument, Santa Bárbara Castle, sits proudly overlooking the sea from the summit of Mount Benacantil. It was first built during the 9th century when Muslims controlled the Iberian Peninsula, but the origins of its name mark the date the castle was captured by Castilian forces on 4 December 1248: the celebration day of Saint Barbara.

Less than half a century later, the Castilian mayor Nicolas Peris faced an uncomfortable decision. Some months previously he had ignored a threatening letter from James II of Aragon demanding he surrender the castle. Now the Aragonese army, which was superior in both weaponry and men, was rapidly closing in. Defeat was inevitable. Yet Peris refused to capitulate, insisting the king would have to fight him one-on-one. As an administrative official he had little hope of winning such a duel and, as expected, when they met his demise was swift. Peris died with a sword in one hand and the keys of the castle in the other. He was holding them so tightly that the only way to take the keys from his lifeless body was to cut off his hand. As one can imagine, James II, infuriated by the indignity and the inconvenience of it all, ordered Peris' body to be fed to the dogs. It is said you can still hear the keys clicking when the ghost of Peris' unburied remains haunt the castle.

The military importance of the castle declined from the 18th century onwards and, as was the case with many other forts, it was subsequently redeployed as a prison. Now the city's most popular tourist attraction, it provides majestic views over the Sierra Grossa, the sea and the rooftops below. Visitors don't even have to walk up the hill to appreciate the scenery, as they can now jump in a lift next to El Postiguet Beach. I passed on the opportunity and opted to hike to the top. I had been cycling for less than a week, but it already felt strange not to be on my bike and halfway to somewhere new. Thus far, I had been pleasantly surprised by my lack of aches and pains. Admittedly, I hadn't been breaking any records with my mileage, but I'd anticipated that I would be feeling the effects of lugging all my paraphernalia in my pannier bags each day. It goes to show how quickly the human body adapts.

Descending from Santa Bárbara Castle I passed through the city's historic Barrio Santa Cruz. Narrow streets zigzagged down the hillside, past small plazas, chapels and colourful houses adorned with decorative pots of flowers. Just as I had the previous day, I spent the afternoon at the beach studying Spanish grammar. Much of my downtime was occupied by this pursuit, but I've avoided mentioning it as the only thing duller than practising Spanish verb conjugations is reading about someone else doing so. It's like watching someone play a computer game, but without any chance of sparking mutual enjoyment from spectacular car crashes, wonder goals or treacherous double agents.

While I was learning, I simultaneously topped up my suntan. It's an endeavour I commit to with fervour each summer. I'm an amateur though compared to the man I saw beside me that afternoon. He was around 40 years old and the colour of a conker. After spending an inordinate amount of time slathering himself in oil, he stood bolt upright in the smallest pair of speedos I've ever seen and proceeded to turn 90° every 15 minutes, timed on his stopwatch. I couldn't help but be impressed by his dedication to attaining an even, full-body tan. His wife lay nearby, but rarely acknowledged him, as if she had long since given up trying to explain it wasn't normal to act as if you're on a rotisserie.

As the temperature began to fall, I visited the second fortress of the day: San Fernando Castle. Built 600 metres inland, it was constructed at the start of the 19th century to help defend the more feted Santa Bárbara Castle from an anticipated attack by the French. The fortification was redundant before it was even completed though as Napoleon reassigned his soldiers to assist his invasion of Russia. Built in haste, San Fernando Castle was soon in a state of disrepair, leaving the city's authorities unsure what to do with it. Two hundred years later, they still haven't decided. So the graffitied remnants of the fort's ramparts remain spread across Mount Tossal, providing a platform for beautiful sunset views, while simultaneously serving as the location for drug deals underneath Alicante's unsightly radio masts.

I had another snatched dinner before returning to the hostel I'd decamped to that morning. The owners of the newly refurbished hostel had gone to great efforts to ensure it had as high a capacity as possible, with the consequence that the rooms were little more than closets of bunk beds and lockers. My room officially slept six but would have been too cramped for more than two people to stand simultaneously. As there were only a handful of guests in the entire hostel, I had the room to myself which was both fortuitous and a little disconcerting.

On the lookout for signs of life, I spent much of the evening sat downstairs in the common room. Disappointingly, there were only a couple of people reading in the dimly lit room and none looked in the mood for a truncated conversation in Spanish.

At precisely 10pm, the receptionist announced abruptly, '*Esta área ya está cerrada. Si queréis quedaros en el hostal, debéis ir a vuestras habitaciones*'. This area is now closed. If you want to stay in the hostel please go to your rooms.

I hadn't been sent to bed so early for years. Steve may have had his faults, but he was more liberal than this.

7

Alicante to Torrevieja

After waking in the silent pitch black of my windowless dormitory, I came down in the morning to the common room to find all the lights switched off. The only person around was a girl with pinched cheeks sitting tucked away in the furthest corner from the sunlight like a vampire. I have mixed feelings about party hostels - what you gain in terms of opportunities to make friends can be outweighed by the lack of sleep - but most libraries have a better atmosphere than this hostel. It was time to move on.

I loaded my pannier bags and set off southwest towards Elche. It wasn't originally part of my itinerary and my knowledge of the place was, like Barnsley in England, limited to the plucky local football team's short-lived stay in the country's top division. I only intended to stop there briefly, but Elche proved an enchanting pit-stop. It's the third largest city in the Valencian region behind Valencia and Alicante. What sets it apart from Barnsley (and anywhere else for that matter) is its palm trees, of which there is the largest number in Europe. Indeed, the city's most famous landmark is the UNESCO World Heritage Site of the Palmeral of Elche, a beguiling park containing more than 200,000 of the trees.

Elche is so close to Alicante that the cities form a de facto conurbation of around 800,000 inhabitants; a figure that doubles during the summer. On the Saturday morning that I arrived there were few tourists around, but the cafes in the plazas were full of life as residents drank coffee and ate churros in the bright morning sunshine. In comparison, the Palmeral of Elche was a haven of serenity. It felt a world away from life in England, where the royal wedding was about to get under way.

The first palm trees in Elche were planted as early as the 5th century BC by the Carthaginians. However, it was the Moors who created the Palmeral of Elche and harvested dates from the trees to feed people and livestock. The site's agricultural use slowly diminished over time and it is now primarily regarded as a cultural asset. Elche's Palm Sunday processions are, predictably, one of the country's most elaborate.

While the Palmeral of Elche may be the city's calling card, its cathedral is almost as impressive. The Basilica of Santa María is a huge stone structure with an eye-catching blue dome. It hosts the annual Mystery Play of Elche, which depicts the death and ascension of the

Virgin Mary. The liturgical drama, first performed in the 15th century, was proclaimed by UNESCO in 2001 as one of the 19 Masterpieces of the Oral and Intangible Heritage of Humanity. Which made me feel bad that I'd never heard of it. A further 71 'masterpieces' were subsequently added to this ostentatiously titled list. It's unlikely to come up in a pub quiz, but you can impress your friends by naming some of the others to make the cut, which include the Albanian Folk Iso-Polyphony, The Woodcrafting Knowledge of the Zafimaniry in Madagascar and the Space of Gong Culture in Vietnam. Start talking about them at length though and you won't have any friends left.

Thankfully, in recent years the grandiose title of Masterpieces of the Oral and Intangible Heritage of Humanity has bitten the dust. It has been replaced by a revised index which now features 508 entries from 122 countries. Curiously, it doesn't include any entry from the UK or the US.

Opposite the cathedral is Altamira Castle. Originally built during the 12th century, the fortress, like Santa Bárbara Castle in Alicante, was used as a prison during the Spanish Civil War. It later became the town hall, but it has since been repurposed once again to host the archaeology and history museum. I'd have happily popped in to learn more about the city, but I'd already stayed far longer in Elche than I had anticipated. So instead I grabbed a selection of pastries from a local bakery, jumped back on the bike and headed south to Torrevieja.

The route took me along quiet, flat roads through the countryside. To break up the journey I stopped again 20km later in San Fulgenico. The compact village seemed to appear out of thin air in the otherwise featureless landscape. According to a recent census, around 16,000 people live here, but I saw no more than four. I assumed everyone had gone to the seaside or were visiting relatives nearby. The truth was less palatable. The same census revealed that 77% of San Fulgenico's population were foreigners, and for many in this demographic, the village would never be home, just the location of their holiday house. It was no wonder the village felt so empty; it would be a couple of months until the majority of its inhabitants arrived.

While San Fulgenico was relatively modest, the elegant village square included numerous carefully sculpted trees. As I looked around from one of the wooden benches in the square, I decided I rather liked the village. I suspected this may have had as much to do with my desire to rest and my enjoyment of the pastries from Elche as anything else though.

As with any long-distance cycle, I spent many hours on my trip pedalling through uninteresting, and sometimes downright monotonous, scenery. What sustained me was the certainty, gleaned after only a couple days of travelling, that it wouldn't be long before I turned a corner and discovered something unusual or unexpectedly pleasing. The salt lagoon of Torrevieja was a perfect example of this. As I approached it, I was confronted by a repugnant eggy, sulphurous smell. Trying not to inhale, I noticed the water had an unmistakable pinkish hue. To begin with, I dismissed this as a sign I needed to breathe, but I then assumed it must be a trick of the light. As it was mid-afternoon and only a few clouds dotted the sky, this seemed improbable. The answer, I found out later, is that the colour is generated by the presence of a specific type of bacteria and algae, which are two of the few organisms able to survive in the highly saline conditions of a man-made salt lake.

At the height of summer, the lagoon is a popular tourist attraction. Many people take a dip in the therapeutic pink waters, while others come to watch the flamingos that gather here. Yet when I passed, the sub-30°C air temperature was evidently insufficient to tempt any would-be swimmers. Due to the high salinity the banks of the lagoon were inert and largely absent of vegetation. Combined with the haphazardly spread salt deposits, the area bore greater resemblance to a contaminated nuclear fallout zone than it did an idyllic holiday destination.

The formation of the salt lake and the neighbouring lagoon helped Torrevieja develop in the 18th century from a little fishing village to a working town. Today, the water sources produce a staggering 700,000 tonnes of salt per year. The city itself is located near the south-eastern end of the lagoon. I stopped to relax at the first beach I found, which was sheltered so effectively by the harbour walls that the sea was almost as placid as the lagoon itself. As a result, the water was noticeably warmer than it had been elsewhere. Less favourably, the stillness of the water made it less effective at washing away toddlers' effluence, the flow of which several parents seemed to actively encourage. I resolved to stay on the shore.

The city has experienced rapid growth in recent decades and is now more than three times the size it was at the start of the 1990s. This increase was overseen by a talented mayor who focused his efforts on developing

Torrevieja's tourism industry. If the tale sounds familiar, there's a twist to this one. After serving as the city's mayor from 1988 to 2012, Pedro Hernández Mateo was sentenced to three years in prison. He was found guilty of prevarication and the falsification of documents concerning the contract for the municipality's rubbish collection service. Having spent years attracting retired Europeans to Torrevieja's beaches, he found himself spending his own retirement in jail, 80km away from the coast.

I explored the city for a while in the evening sun, before going to meet my host. I knew I was in roughly the right place, but finding the front door was no easy task and I felt as if I was looking for a speakeasy as I paced up and down the street.

'*Debe ser Chris,*' said a voice from behind me. You must be Chris.

I turned round to see a couple and a young boy pushing bicycles along the pavement.

'*Lamento llegar tarde, salimos a pasear en bici.*' Sorry we're late - we were on a bike ride.

I took a shine to them immediately.

The man introduced himself as Guillermo and we quickly fell into a lengthy discussion in Spanish about my ride so far and the joy of cycling in the cool evening temperatures. It was wonderful to have someone to talk to after spending hours with only my own thoughts for company and it wasn't long before I was asking to stay another night.

I was wary of the danger of focusing on the miles I accomplished each day, rather than the journey itself. In an effort to guard against this, I'd promised myself I would dwell in places that warranted it. Truth be told, I'm not sure Torrevieja fitted that category, but I enjoyed a rest day studying Spanish and hunting for prospective jobs to start upon my return to England. In any event, I steered clear of entering the water.

8

Torrevieja to Murcia

Early the next morning I left Guillermo's flat to cycle to Murcia. It represented a significant detour inland, but I was looking forward to meeting Luis, a language exchange friend with whom I had met on a weekly basis in London for a couple of years before I flew to Panama. After running out of money, he had temporarily come back to his hometown just outside of Murcia. Luis is unlike anyone I've ever met. Quiet, considerate and scrupulously fair, he holds few principles, but holds them with a vice-like grip. He has no interest in sport and considers it to be a 'distraction for the proletariat'. This assessment is an indication of both his left-wing politics and his dexterity in English. He's also a passionate vegan and a conspiracy theorist who believes governments around the world regularly allow atrocities to occur to suit their own ends.

While this provided unexpected opportunities to learn new vocabulary, it somewhat inevitably led to occasional disagreements between us. When Luis had shared his opinion that the 9/11 terror attacks were orchestrated by the Bush administration, my incredulity and limited grasp of Spanish had prevented me from questioning his rationale and I'd been forced to splutter my response in English. Nevertheless, I was excited to see a familiar face and I was eager to demonstrate how my language skills had improved during my time away.

Before I began the day's cycling in earnest, I stopped for what was intended to be a tranquil breakfast on a beach heading out of Torrevieja. Regrettably, I was spotted by a drunken Spaniard who began to serenade me with an incoherent dirge as he approached. I kept hoping he'd stop, but his 'singing' became more belligerent with every passing minute. In the end a drunken British man, collapsed face down in the sand about 50 metres away, told him in no uncertain terms to shut up. Inebriated Brits abroad have a poor reputation, but his explicit, unequivocal intervention echoed my sentiments perfectly.

Tiptoeing around my fellow countryman, I began cycling to Murcia via La Pedrera Reservoir. After cycling through the region's parched, barren hills, the gleaming turquoise water appeared suddenly like an oasis. Built in 1980 to help irrigate the local farmland, the reservoir's importance is self-evident from the fertility of the nearby fields. Under a clear blue sky, the wide road around the reservoir's perimeter provided beautiful views and the only traffic I came across were from like-minded individuals on bicycles and motorbikes. At the north-western side of the reservoir I reluctantly turned off, resuming my cycle through agrarian countryside until I reached the eastern suburbs of Murcia.

As Spain's seventh largest city, Murcia had far more to offer than merely play host to my catch up with Luis. I followed the Segura River to the cathedral in the centre of the city, where the heart and the entrails of King Alfonso X were buried under the main altar. Alfonso requested this as a demonstration of his love for Murcia and his gratitude to the fidelity that the city's residents showed him. He exhibited rather less to his wife, fathering several illegitimate children. One of these came from an affair with his aunt, making his daughter his niece. In spite of this incestuous behaviour, the king was nicknamed Alfonso the Wise and his reign between 1221 and 1284 coincided with significant intellectual progress in the fields of science, literature and law. You do have to question the wisdom of a man though who married a 13-year-old girl and then viewed her as infertile when she failed to produce an heir during their first four years of marriage. In adulthood she proved the fallacy of those early preconceptions, going on to have 11 children in 13 years.

That morning I had received a succession of voice messages over WhatsApp from my next Airbnb host. I had hoped to meet her in person, but our interactions were conducted entirely remotely. Each missive I received, expressed at the speed of sound, contained important instructions. My listening skills, which were never the strongest, were put to the test as I was first told to speak to a nearby restaurant owner to pick up the keys. I then had to follow a convoluted set of directions to reach the property. Upon entering the building, I found a large empty flat with a number of bedrooms, and ascertained, as best I could, which was the only one I was permitted to enter. I felt like *Alice in Wonderland* trapped in the Room of Doors. I needed to rewind each message countless times before I was confident enough to face the next stage of this elaborate treasure hunt, where the prize was a bed for the night for which I'd already paid.

Eventually I found the treasure: a bare mattress with the accompanying linen laid next to the pillow. Before I could be informed it was the wrong bed, I deposited my stuff on top of it and headed out to the Malecón Gardens. The park hosts the city's botanical gardens so I anticipated coming across a verdant plot of land, but the gardens consisted only of wide walkways separating islands of small, plain flower beds. I like my botanical gardens to have a bit more botany, so I didn't stay for long.

Further along the riverbank, there is a memorial to Juan de la Cierva, who is widely acknowledged to be one of the most important figures in Spanish aviation history. Cierva invented the gyroplane, the predecessor of the modern helicopter. Unlike a helicopter, which uses an engine to power its spinning blades, a gyroplane's blades turn purely as a result of the flow of air from below. In 1928 a prototype of his design successfully flew from London to Paris, becoming the first rotating wing aircraft to cross the Channel. Tragically, he died in a plane crash in Croydon just eight years later. In total 15 people lost their lives in the incident, which at the time was the UK's worst ever air crash.

I crossed one of the many bridges and explored the area south of the river. This part of the city has fewer tourist sites, but includes the historic Garden of Floridablanca. Shaped like a slice of cake between three intersecting roads, it was Spain's first public park and has become a symbol of Murcia. By now the sun had sunk out of sight behind the buildings so I returned towards the cathedral in Plaza del Cardenal Belluga. I did so with the aim of practising some verb conjugations, but ostensibly it was to people watch while I ate dinner.

9

Murcia

I had agreed to meet Luis in the afternoon so I should have permitted myself a lazy morning. Instead, curiosity got the better of me and I cycled out of town on a 25km round trip to visit Our Lady of Fuensanta Sanctuary. Located in El Valle y Carrascoy park, the 17th century temple was built to honour the patron saint of Murcia, the Virgin of Fuensanta.

Visiting the sanctuary is promoted online as a refreshing day out, yet negotiating a way through the heavy traffic of the city's choked road network was anything but. The sanctuary was built on a steep hillside and is the wedding venue of choice for wealthy Murcians. It's not hard to see why. Surrounded by pine forest, the sanctuary's elegant white towers have sweeping views over the nearby vineyards and clay tennis courts, with the city and the distant mountains contributing to a magnificent backdrop.

As with so many religious buildings, the exterior surpassed anything inside. Excitable school children swarmed between the pews, so I didn't linger and instead cycled around some of the park's 16,000 undulating hectares. The narrow road through the woodland featured several sharp bends and stone bridges passing over small streams. It didn't really lead anywhere, just higher and higher up the hill, and as a consequence attracted little traffic. Liberated from the weight of the pannier bags which I had left in my room, I felt like a rally driver as I joyfully threw my bike around each corner. The park is home to wild cats and snakes, but apart from the occasional bird of prey, I didn't see a thing. Having got my rush of adrenaline for the day, I turned back and ate lunch from a spot overlooking the sanctuary.

I returned to the city to meet up with Luis in the Plaza del Cardenal Belluga. It was good to see him. After spending so much time by myself, it was nice not to feel compelled to force a conversation in Spanish at every opportunity, but to use it simply to chat to an old friend. We spoke for an hour in Spanish before swapping to English as Luis divulged his latest theory.

'Did you know pharmaceutical companies are secretly encouraged to test experimental medication on orphans in Africa to ensure drugs are safe for Europeans?' he asked me.

'No, I didn't,' I replied.

'It's true - thousands of children have suffered terrible

side effects and many have died.'

'I don't think that could be kept secret,' I said. 'It would be too big a story.'

I'd fallen right into the conspiracist's trap.

'Don't trust the mainstream media,' Luis intoned, 'there are other, better informed publications online.'

I wanted to tell him not to believe everything he read on conspiracy101.com, but I held my tongue. Just as there is no point arguing with someone with opposing beliefs about Brexit, arguing with conspiracy theorists is a waste of time. You can't change their opinion and only succeed in leading them to become exasperated by your own.

Conversation turned to more amiable topics, such as the local controversy regarding the extension to the city hall which stood to our right. The Modernist design of the building juxtaposes the baroque architecture of the cathedral it faces across the plaza. Normally, I would have approved of the decision to mix such contrasting styles, but we both admitted the extension's stone facade bore an unfavourable resemblance to a wooden IKEA shelving unit that was missing a few parts.

My desire to hear Luis' assessment of my Spanish was playing on my mind. I had no doubt I'd improved during the eight months since we'd last met, but Luis was the only person who could judge this with authority. While I considered some of his political views absurd, I trusted his opinion on other topics and I knew he would be honest in his appraisal. I took a deep breath.

'So what do you think of my Spanish?' I asked as casually as I could.

Luis was good enough not to tease me on the transparent neediness of the question. I knew whatever he said next would rattle around my head for several days.

'You are definitely better than you were. Conversation flows much better now you know more of the verb tenses. Just keep practising,' he said with a smile.

I breathed a sigh of relief, pleased with this qualified praise.

When Luis left to go home, I explored the streets of Murcia's commercial area. The late afternoon sun shone brightly, but couldn't penetrate the narrow, centuries-old streets. Their comparative darkness was exacerbated by a high canvas that ran the length of the Calle Traperia to protect pedestrians both from rain and the summer sun. At the end of the street I stepped blinking into the sunlight that bathed the Plaza Santo Domingo.

Today the plaza is filled with cafes and public benches, but in 1824 it was the execution site of the wonderfully named Jaime the Bearded. Jaime's life reads like a Hollywood movie. Initially an honest family man, he fled to the mountains to escape the law and inevitable reprisals after he killed a bandit while guarding his father's field. Portraying himself as a Valencian Robin Hood, he rapidly gained popular support. This multiplied when he deployed his skills against Napoleon's invading army. Jaime received a pardon in recognition for his efforts during the conflict, but, unable to leave his past behind, he subsequently returned to his old life as an outlaw. Eventually he was betrayed and brought to justice. Not content with sending him to the gallows, the authorities ordered for Jaime's body to be dismembered and his offal fried and sent across the region to deter others from following in his footsteps.

Back at the apartment, I found I'd gained a fellow lodger. A middle-aged French woman had successfully negotiated our Airbnb host's complex clues to enter the building, but was clearly bemused by the process and unsure, as I had been, about which of the rooms was allocated to her. I empathised, but my failed attempts to express this merely underlined my complete lack of French. Still, one language at a time, I guess.

10

Murcia to Cartagena

The houses of suburban Murcia quickly thinned out, replaced first by grey hills and then by wide dusty plains as I travelled due south. It was far from the most interesting scenery of the trip, but I was grateful for the flat terrain.

I had just resigned myself to the fact that this inland stretch would remain characterless, when I unexpectedly joined up with a narrow canal of turquoise water. Approximately two metres wide, the canal is supplied by La Pedrera Reservoir and runs for 64km like a blue ribbon across the landscape. My own route ran parallel to it for 9km, during which time I saw only one person: a farmer and his dog shepherding sheep. Trying to find a way past a hundred skittish sheep on a path the width of a car was as challenging as it sounds. The banks of the canal didn't have any barriers, so I worried my approach from behind the flock would cause the sheep to topple over the edge in panic, in much the same way as Gabriel Oak's herd in *Far From The Madding Crowd*.

I carefully squeezed past, putting myself between the livestock and the canal where possible. A few kilometres further on I arrived at a road junction that would take me into Cartagena. The only problem was that access to the road from the canal path was blocked by a pumping station encircled by a high metal fence. I was desperate to avoid backtracking to find an alternative route, not least because I knew the farmer would be far from impressed if he saw me again. I ruled out the idea of scaling the fence - I realised that I'd never be able to get my bike over it - and was relieved when I found a concealed path bordering the garden of a nearby house that led me to the road.

Cycling through rural landscapes is almost always more enjoyable than pedalling your way through a city. It's just as well too, as the majority of the time spent on long-distance cycles is in remote countryside. Still, there is something undeniably exciting about returning to civilization. The number of buildings increase, to borrow Ernest Hemingway's phrase, 'at first slowly, then suddenly' as cities draw you in to their chaotic, noisy and polluted embrace. Initially, outlets of international shopping brands appear in out-of-town retail parks, then, approaching the centre, attractive public gardens and local landmarks pique the curiosity.

My bed for the night was a 20-minute walk north of the harbour. My host, Sofia, was more perfunctory than friendly, but at least she was there to meet me. I didn't know anything about Cartagena, but I was pleased to be back by the sea, in a city full of history. I began by walking down Calle Real towards the Arsenal of Cartagena, where I anticipated seeing some of the weapons used over the centuries to defend the city. The striking yellow tower at the entrance hinted at the site's storied past, but the huge closed wooden doors and the seven-metre high white walls that ran far into the distance in both directions made it abundantly clear that visitors were not welcome. I later learned the Arsenal of Cartagena is home to Spain's naval headquarters in the Mediterranean, so it's understandable the complex doesn't open its doors for tourists to have a mosey.

Cartagena is noticeably different from the other towns and cities along the coastline, all of which are built around the seasonal influx of sun-seeking tourists. It has a comparative paucity of local sandy beaches and instead it relies, with admittedly mixed results, on its 3,000 years of history to attract visitors. Much of the city felt empty and it exuded a different, heavier atmosphere than the jaunty coastal resorts I had travelled through in recent days.

Once again curious as to where everyone was, I visited Concepción Castle, one of Cartagena's main tourist attractions. Built on top of a hill, the historical site has an impressive view of the neighbouring Roman amphitheatre, the waterfront and the suburbs inland. In its heyday the amphitheatre held more than 6,000 people and was dedicated to Gaius and Lucius Caesar, the grandsons of Augustus, the first Roman emperor. When the pair were young, Augustus named them as his eventual successors, but they both predeceased him.

First Lucius fell ill in Marseille while travelling to visit the Roman army in southern Spain. Less than a month later, his brother Gaius fell for the oldest trick in the book when he accepted a personal invitation to visit the headquarters of the enemy nationalist forces in Armenia. Aged just 21 years old, Gaius' naivety cost him his life. He was attacked and suffered fatal injuries.

This left Augustus with a headache over who should take his place. He chose his stepson Tiberius, along with Gaius and Lucius' younger brother, Postumus. Within two years Augustus had removed Postumus from the line of succession and had forced him to live in exile on Pianosa, a remote island located between Corsica and Italy's west coast. He never saw his grandfather again.

The precise reasons for Augustus' change of opinion are unclear, but it seems he was dissuaded of his grandson's suitability. According to the Roman politician Tacitus, Postumus was 'devoid of every good quality', while historian Erich S. Gruen described him as a 'vulgar young man, brutal and brutish, and of depraved character'. Such traits haven't prevented others from running for high office though.

As Augustus lay on his deathbed eight years later, Postumus was killed, allegedly on the instructions of his step-brother and soon to be emperor, Tiberius. In a superb plot twist, Postumus' slave Clemens impersonated his former master and quickly gained a following. The resemblance between the two men was slight, but Clemens benefitted from the public's inability to recall Postumus' appearance after he had spent so long in exile. Seizing his opportunity, Clemens took his swelling ranks of supporters to Rome with the avowed intention of inheriting the sovereignty held by his 'grandfather'. This ambition was thwarted when individuals loyal to Tiberius infiltrated the group. Clemens was captured and tortured to death.

At the top of Concepción Castle, I saw one other person admiring the 360° views. She was a short woman in her early sixties who had dyed maroon hair and wore big sunglasses that the weather didn't really warrant. As I turned to look at the scenery, she began to angrily reprimand me in a language I didn't recognise. I began walking slowly towards her barrage of invective to see if I could find out and apologise for whatever heinous mistake I had committed. It was only when I was less than two metres away that she abruptly stopped in her tracks, presumably because she realised I wasn't her husband. As someone who has benefitted hugely from laser eye surgery, I understand the difficulties caused by short sightedness. Even so, I found it a little odd that she would mistake me for her partner. In my red shorts and hideous green jumper I resembled a 14-year-old skateboarder dressed like a Christmas tree.

11

Cartagena

The following day, I fast forwarded almost 2,000 years of history and visited the city's fascinating Civil War Museum. The Spanish Civil War lasted from 1936 to 1939 and pitted Republicans against Nationalists.

Republicans were on the side of the government and consisted of a coalition of democrats, anarchists, socialists and communists. The limited international support they received came from volunteers and the Soviet Union. On the other side were the Nationalist rebels, led by General Franco, who formed an alliance between conservatives, monarchists, nationalists and fascists. Although the rebels received assistance from both Adolf Hitler and Benito Mussolini, Britain, France and the US adopted a policy of non-intervention in an attempt to avoid the conflict escalating into World War II.

Cartagena's population sided with the elected, left-leaning Second Spanish Republic. It paid a heavy price for its loyalty. The city was a major munitions production centre and its port served as both the base for the Republican fleet and the access point for foreign aid. Franco knew that if he was able to seize control of Cartagena, other Republican areas north of the city would fall soon after. However, the city's military defences were extensive, thanks to the litany of armed conflicts it had witnessed throughout history. This made it difficult to capture by land or sea and led the Nationalists to focus their efforts on bringing the city to its knees through aerial bombardment. Residents responded by constructing air raid shelters and the Civil War Museum is located in one of the largest. Dug deep into the slope of Monte de la Concepción, the shelter was capable of protecting 5,500 people.

Cartagena's anti-aircraft guns forced the Nationalist planes to fly higher and drop bombs less accurately, but the city still suffered widespread damage. This was in spite of the ingenious efforts of some individuals, who attached lights to hundreds of poles in fields outside of the city. During night-time air raids, the city turned off all the lights and switched on those in the fields, drawing the attention of the pilots, who dropped their bombs innocuously over farmland. Eventually, the city fell to the Nationalists and just a day later, on 1 April 1939, Franco delivered his victory speech as the remaining Republican fighters surrendered across the country.

In total half a million people died during the civil war

and nearly 1,500 of those perished in a single incident just off the shore of Cartagena in 1939. Franco had ordered 30 transporters and warships to converge on the city in the hope of forcing the weary citizens to capitulate. The Republican forces resisted the attack and all but one of the ships beat a hasty retreat to safety. Hindered by broken radio communications and a top speed of just 10 knots, the *Castillo de Olite* limped behind the rest of the fleet and broke in two after sustaining a direct hit. The immense loss of life was utterly futile; just 25 days later the rebels claimed victory and Franco swept to power.

12

Cartagena to Vera

There were no obvious places to stop between Cartagena and Almería, the next major city along the coast, so with more than 200km separating the two, I'd reserved a room in a town as close to equidistant as I could get. Appropriately for a place that's both old and no longer in vogue, its name was Vera.

I began the day cycling south-west along the Carretera de Tentegorra, an inviting 3km pine tree-lined avenue that took me directly from Cartagena to the nature reserve of the Sierra de la Muela, Cabo Tiñoso y Roldán. I gradually ascended over the next 20km until I arrived at a summit, where I looked back triumphantly at the road winding between the hills I had just travelled across and ahead to the sandy bay at Isla Plana below.

There was barely a car in sight on the descent, allowing me to ride the hairpin bends with carefree, if not quite careless, abandon. When the final turn revealed a long, sweeping slope I made the most of the momentum I had gained from losing 300 metres of altitude in less than a minute. The 100kg combined weight of my pannier bags, my bike and myself quickly propelled me to more than 60km/h. Heavy pannier bags transform a bicycle into a steam train: slow to pick up speed, but when heading downhill, almost impossible to catch.

As I picked up speed, my eyes streamed and salty tears ran down my cheeks. I couldn't have felt happier, for there are few better feelings than looking forward to eating a well-earned breakfast while rapidly descending on a bike towards an unexplored beach.

Perhaps inevitably, the village of Isla Plana was a disappointment and failed to match my imagination's exalted expectations. It consisted predominantly of unoccupied holiday homes, so I only paused briefly to eat an orange and some nuts before I resumed cycling.

The beauty of the beaches increased as I continued heading west and it soon became difficult to resist stopping for another break. My little remaining willpower disappeared when a yellow, otherworldly rock formation appeared just outside of Salado. This, I learned, was the Enchanted City of Bolnuevo. While the description of the site as a 'city' was something of a misnomer, the peculiar, 30-metre high gravity-defying giant fungi-like shapes of the sandstone rocks were undeniably intriguing and a consequence of thousands of years of wind and water erosion.

From here I entered the Sierra de las Moreras, which

translates as the Mulberry Tree Mountains. Mulberrys, for those unfamiliar with the fruit, resemble elongated blackberries. Despite passing through the area, I had to look this up as the region suffered from such extensive deforestation during the 16th century that there is no longer a mulberry tree in sight - just rocky hills covered by small grasses. My decision to buy a road bike over a mountain bike had already been vindicated - I had barely made it up some of the hills as it was - but the road's disintegration into a stony track here was the first time I had cause to worry for the longevity of my tyres.

The path skirted numerous sandy coves such as the popular nudist spot Wolf Cave Beach. The shimmering blue water beckoned, but I kept my clothes on and proceeded on my bike as carefully as I could until the path disappeared entirely at the edge of a forgotten dirty shoreline strewn with seaweed. The relief that my tyres had survived the 3km of rough terrain to get to this point was tempered by the need to push my bike through the deep grey sand. At the earliest opportunity I turned inland and became lost in a maze of industrial polythene farming tents, each of which housed hundreds of tomato plants.

I quickly grew frustrated as one dead end followed another. By now I was ravenous and urgently needing to replenish my depleted water reserves. The heat of the midday sun was intense and beads of sweat were rolling down my face at a rate faster than I could drink to replace them.

Half an hour later, I found a way onto the main road and saw for the first time the daunting height of the mountain that lay before me. The biggest climb of my trip so far couldn't have come at a worse time. In my current state there was more chance of someone boring a tunnel through it that afternoon than there was of me cycling over the top of it. I had bonked.

Bonking is the unfortunate term used by cyclists to describe the listlessness riders experience when they have failed to eat enough food to replace the calories they've expended. With their energy levels hovering around zero, they become sluggish and lightheaded. Neither elite athletes nor casual hobbyists are immune to bonking and once it sets in, it takes time to return to normal performance levels. It's why ironman competitors spend almost as much time eating as they do exercising during a race.

As I came round a bend, my spirits were raised considerably by the unexpected sight of a small Spar supermarket. There were so few houses nearby it could hardly have been profitable, but it had a happy customer in me. The woman at the till, the only person in the shop, watched with some amusement as I walked excitedly through the doors into the cool, air-conditioned store. I bought a baguette, a large pack of sliced cheese and a couple of bananas. Too exhausted to find a more scenic spot, I ate them greedily in the store's empty car park, which was big enough only for two vehicles. I filled up my bottles from the tap on the wall, drinking as much as I could and throwing some over my head for good measure. I then re-filled my bottles with three litres of water, adding 3kg of unwelcome weight to my bike. As the weeks went by I began not to top the bottles up to the brim mid-ride in order to reduce my load, gambling I would find another water source before they ran out. It didn't always pay off.

I waited for a while to regain my energy, idly watching a large delivery lorry arrive and attempt a wildly ambitious three-point turn on the narrow road. Seeing he would be there some time, and probably still is now, I set off to conquer the mountain. A series of switchbacks left my calves screaming in agony. Each bend in the road only revealed another distant summit ahead. When I did get to the peak, I felt little joy - just grim satisfaction. I tried to find the little Spar to see where I had come from, but it was hidden amongst the rolling hills of the Sierra de las Moreras, which ran for as far as the eye could see. Turning to my direction of travel, I could behold the vast blue expanse of the sea and the steep downhill that would take me to the plain next to it.

The journey down was even more spectacular than the day's earlier descent. Sadly, I was inhibited by the inopportune realisation that something had gone awry with my front brake. I apprehensively returned to sea level, pumping the brakes at regular intervals to slow my speed in case they failed altogether and sent me hurtling towards the rock face or, alternatively, straight over the precipice. At the bottom of the slope the empty road lay invitingly before me. But I felt shortchanged. In preparation for the next downhill section, I set about fixing the brake, deliberately ignoring my memories of previous experiences that underlined my limitations in this department.

The situation quickly unravelled. When I removed a screw no more than 5mm long that had been fitted close to the handle, the brake went from problematic to utterly useless. I spent the next 25 minutes trying to put the screw back, a job that would have been easier for someone with far more slender fingers than my own. Once again, I couldn't help but think of Sarah. Both her degree in engineering and her dainty digits would have been far more useful than any skill I possessed. Even when I'd managed to replace the screw, the brake was still much worse than it had been prior to my cack-handed effort to repair it.

Thwarted by my own ineptitude, I carried on before I could do any more damage. Having cycled the thankfully flat 10km towards Águilas, I fortuitously came across an out-of-town Decathlon store. The staff, equipped with both the tools and knowhow I lacked, fixed my brake with the minimum of fuss. I felt like a Formula 1 driver who had pulled into the pits. Consequently, even if Águilas had resembled a dystopian nightmare, I would recall it fondly. Rose-tinted glasses were unnecessary though; it really was a pretty town and featured a hilltop castle overlooking the sea.

As I was short on time, I wasn't able to explore the castle, so I admired it from one end of the sandy bay below. While I tucked into some more of the rations I'd purchased at Spar, I watched locals in their early teens enjoying themselves on the beach. Travelling across the country, I was repeatedly struck by the difference between my own upbringing and that of Spanish adolescents who lived near the coast. Here, groups of boys and girls frolicked on the shore in swimming trunks and bikinis. The boys grabbing the girls, threatening, and sometimes gleefully committing, to throw them into the sea and the girls reacting with ear-splitting shrieks. These interactions were in sharp contrast to my experiences at a similar age. Other than during occasional school swimming lessons, teenage girls and boys in Britain scarcely see each others' bodies going through the vagaries of puberty, yet Spain's beach culture means there is no hiding place. Even when the groups of boys and girls were apart, there was no doubt that the boys were watching the girls. And boy, did the girls know it.

I could have happily stayed in Águilas for longer, but I still had 40km to go until I made it to Vera and the shadows were already lengthening. In my haste to grind out some miles, my navigating went awry.

Sometimes on the bike it was easier to just keep riding and hope for the best, than to pause at every junction. When I retraced my journey on the map in the process of writing this book, I was amused by the extraordinary number of times I had inadvertently diverted from each day's intended course.

Shortly after reaching the village of Los Lobos (The Wolves), I made a howling error. Instead of taking a direct backroad to Vera, I ended up on a longer route on the hard shoulder of a dual carriageway. Luckily, the only cars on the road were on the other side of the central reservation, their headlights twinkling in the fading light as they passed. It was by now nearly 10pm and I was hungry, tired and impatient for the remaining kilometres to disappear. Not for the last time, I had bitten off more than I could chew.

Vera is a small town of around 16,000 people. Its claim to fame, limited as it is, comes from its reputation as a centre for naturism. This was cemented in 2013 when the town's nudists entered the Guinness Book of World

Records after smashing the record for the largest ever skinny dip.

Such achievements were far from my mind as I crawled my way into the town. I passed the Church of the Incarnation, which, in contrast to the rest of the town's dark streets, was lit up like a Christmas tree. When the previous structure was destroyed by an earthquake in the 16th century, King Carlos I ordered a more robust construction to replace it. It needed to not only be able to withstand natural disasters, but attacks from Mediterranean pirates too. As a result, the finished article bears greater resemblance to a fortress than a church. The windows are little more than arrow slits and the building had internal access to an underground aquifer, in case the town's residents were besieged.

King Carlos I, also known as Charles V of the Holy Roman Empire, was an interesting character, as one might expect with parents called Philip the Handsome and Joanna the Mad. Neither gifted with his father's piercing blue eyes, nor afflicted by his mother's mental illness, he had several mistresses, one of whom was his step-grandmother. While it probably made family reunions tense affairs, in his defence she was 29 at the time and they were only 12 years apart.

Back in the present, my curiosity had been somewhat dulled by the cycle and I longed for a bed to collapse into. To my disappointment, my host Benito wasn't at home, but returned from a late night run 15 minutes later, full of restless energy. His tall, wiry frame didn't have an inch of fat, suggesting he went running most nights.

'*¿Quiere unirse a mis amigos y yo para cenar?* Do you want to join my friends and I for dinner?

My weary limbs were more than happy to stay just where they were, but I realised this was the type of offer I should jump at. Desperate for sustenance and knowing I'd wonder in the morning what I might have missed, I acceded.

After struggling to hold myself back from bankrupting myself while ordering tapas, I chatted to Benito's friends and tried to keep up with their conversations. Unfortunately, I just wasn't at the races. Even so, I couldn't help but notice the suspiciously intimate relationship Benito appeared to have with his best friend's long-term girlfriend. Benito's best friend, Jorge, seemed oblivious to this but I predicted he would have a rude awakening sooner rather than later.

When I couldn't hide my fatigue any longer, Benito decided we should probably make a move. He had no intention of going home though and insisted we visit the white statue of Jesus at the top of a hill on the western outskirts of Vera.

Jorge tagged along too and having parked the car nearby, we began walking up a spiral path to the statue at the summit. I learned subsequently that the statue receives few visitors during the day, so inevitably, there was no one else on the hill at midnight. The path was lit only by sporadic lampposts and I began to feel uneasy. I had met Benito and Jorge barely two hours ago and now, purely out of politeness, I found myself alone with them in the dark on a remote, windy hill.

My companions appeared relaxed, but the night now felt sinister as I realised how vulnerable I was. I knew I wouldn't stand much chance against the two of them if they did wish me ill. Somewhat ridiculously, I made sure to walk behind them to conceal my anxiety and ensure I kept them both in sight. I told myself that there wasn't anything to be worried about, and that this really was just a fun excursion. However, I couldn't shake off the thought that if you were planning to rob someone, wouldn't you do it in the dead of night, where you knew no one would be, with your friend to offer back up if necessary? As we continued to walk in ascending circles around the hill, I wondered what awaited me at the top, when I would be furthest from safety. It felt like an inverted version of the painting of Dante's *Inferno*, with each step up the hill one closer to impending doom.

At the peak Benito and Jorge talked about the town's landmarks. My mind was racing and I failed to take much in as I looked at the lights shining below. Only the story of how the statue had been decapitated by lightning seven years before registered with me. I can't think why.

We stayed up there for what felt like an age. Try as I might, I couldn't work out how, without walking backwards, I could lead the others down the hill while simultaneously keeping them in vision. Finally, we set off back towards the car and returned home at 2.30am. I had been wrong; there was no malice aforethought. It just shows how perceptions can change when darkness falls. To an overtired brain, anything - even a stroll to see a local attraction - can feel portentous.

13

Vera to Almería

Still unsettled by the (non) events of the night before, when I woke I was pleased to find my wallet untouched and my limbs attached. Which always helps when you're about to jump on a bike. I was keen to arrive in Almería that evening in good time as the Champions League final, featuring Liverpool and Real Madrid, was set to take place and I rather fancied watching the game in a beach bar with a beer in hand. So I chose to forgo exploring Vera in daylight and hit the road instead. I cycled to the coast and travelled through a couple of delightful seaside towns just south of Palomares. The name may not ring any bells, but what happened there on 17 January 1966 could have stopped bells ringing forever.

That day a US aircraft carrying four hydrogen bombs,

each 70 times more powerful than the atomic bomb dropped on Hiroshima, collided with another plane during mid-air refuelling. In total, seven of the 11 people aboard the planes died. The bomber carrying the explosives disintegrated and the bombs fell from the skies above Palomares. The non-nuclear explosives in two of the weapons detonated upon impact, resulting in plutonium contamination of a 2km area. The third bomb was found intact, but the location of the fourth remained a mystery. The countryside was painstakingly searched for several days to no avail until the authorities were forced to reluctantly accept that the bomb had landed in the sea. A Spanish sailor called Francisco Simo Orts, henceforth known as Bomb Frankie, had said as much from the start as he was out at sea when he saw the bomb enter the water.

Belatedly, the US launched what, at the time, was the greatest maritime search in history. Not only were American officials racing to limit the potential radioactive fallout, but they were also preoccupied by the possibility that the bomb would be discovered by lurking Soviet boats. If this happened, the White House feared the Soviets would salvage the weapon, learn US military secrets and gain a crucial advantage in the escalating nuclear arms race. New evidence uncovered in the weeks prior to the publication of this book revealed the threat of nuclear espionage lay closer to home though. Franco was eager for Spain to develop its own nuclear programme, which was codenamed Project Islero. In the immediate aftermath of the accident, he ordered the country's scientists to discreetly collect fragments of the hydrogen bombs so that the technology could be replicated in Spanish laboratories.

To find the bomb that had landed in the sea, the US Navy deployed an innovative technique called Bayesian Theory to estimate the probability of where the bomb lay on the seabed. Today, Bayesian Theory is helping to unlock the potential of artificial intelligence, but back then it was nascent technology and it took two months before the bomb was found. In the process of retrieving it, the US Navy dropped the bomb and lost it again. They had in their hands one of the most powerful weapons the world had ever seen, but like a child grabbing a toy while playing on the electric claw game in an arcade, they let it slip from their grasp. It was another 16 days before it was found again.

Once the bomb had been located, Bomb Frankie appeared in court in New York with his lawyer to claim salvage rights. It is custom in maritime law for an individual who provides information leading to the successful recovery of goods lost at sea to receive a reward equivalent to around 1% of the salvaged item's value. This was the last thing the US military, already deeply embarrassed by the incident, needed. US Secretary of Defence Robert McNamara had previously valued each bomb at $2 billion, leaving Bomb Frankie in line to receive $20 million. The US Air Force settled out of court for an undisclosed sum, but Bomb Frankie later complained he never received the money.

The fact that the accident didn't cause far greater damage was in large part due to the effectiveness of the fail-safe systems in the hydrogen bombs. Still, many echoed the sentiments of a Soviet official who stated,

'Only a fortunate stroke of luck saved the Spanish population of the area from catastrophe'.

On the frontline of this narrowly averted nuclear disaster was Carl Brashear. A handsome man with a round face and well-groomed moustache, he was the first African-American diver in the US Navy. During the operation to recover the warhead he was injured in a freak accident and had to have his lower left leg amputated. Two years later, Brashear resumed his duties after becoming the first amputee to be (re)certified as a diver in the navy. His stellar career was depicted in the 2000 Hollywood movie *Men of Honor*, featuring Robert de Niro and Cuba Gooding Jr.

The underlying question to the whole episode is why was a plane carrying four hydrogen bombs over Spain in the first place? The answer lies in Operation Chrome Dome. This was an ambitious US programme, initiated in 1960, to ensure there was always a small number of aircraft carrying thermonuclear weapons en route to the Soviet Union in case the president ordered an attack against the Communist state. One might think that an international crisis such as the one sparked by the crash above Palomares would lead officials to reassess whether such a hazardous operation was strictly necessary. However, it wasn't the first tragedy connected to the programme and sadly it wasn't the last. In spite of the fact that 14 people died in four separate incidents involving planes carrying 10 atomic weapons, Operation Chrome Dome remained in place until 1968. It was only terminated when non-nuclear explosives again detonated upon impact when a B-52 crashed onto the ice in Greenland.

The US consistently downplayed the significance of these events. While the fourth hydrogen bomb was still missing following the crash over Palomares, Spain's information and tourism minister Manuel Fraga and US ambassador Angier Biddle Duke sought to reassure locals and holidaymakers that it was perfectly safe to enter the water. It wasn't. The two men risked exposing themselves to unhealthy levels of radiation while posing for photos as they swam in the Mediterranean. Duke told reporters glibly, 'If this is radioactivity, I love it.' Neither man turned into the Hulk and both lived long and full lives; Fraga passed away at the grand old age of 89, while Duke died at 79 after being struck by a car while rollerblading. Many of those who helped to remove the worst of the plutonium were not so lucky.

It's worth pausing to discuss Manuel Fraga in more detail here. A man with a famously short temper, although he didn't turn green, many Spaniards considered him a monster. More than anything, he was a political survivor, and the only member of Franco's fascist government still in active politics in the 21st century. Yet his career was nearly over before it had really begun. Not long after being appointed the country's information and tourism minister, he accidentally shot Franco's daughter in the bottom during a hunt. Even this didn't halt his rise. Her father simply commented, 'people who can't shoot straight shouldn't come'.

Fraga may have been a terrible shot, but he wasn't afraid of getting others to do the shooting. Early in his career he authorised the execution of several political prisoners, yet by the mid-1960s he was attempting to establish himself as a reformist. In 1966 he loosened some censorship laws, leading to the popular expression 'Con Fraga hasta la braga' (With Fraga [you can see] even knickers). As Spain's dictator aged, Fraga carefully cultivated a public image for himself as the progressive face of Francoism and was appointed home secretary shortly after Franco died.

The mask of liberalism quickly slipped. Fraga's belief that towns and cities belonged to the state as opposed to its citizens, was perfectly encapsulated by his outburst '¡La calle es mía!' (The streets are mine!). In one notorious incident, protestors in the Basque city of Vitoria-Gasteiz clashed with police. When the 4,000 demonstrators retreated into a church, Fraga ordered officers to storm the building. Five fleeing protestors were shot dead and more than 100 others were wounded.

Such an event would ruin most political careers, but the following year Fraga was selected to be one of the Fathers of the new Spanish constitution that was approved in 1978. Fraga also co-founded, along with other former Francoist ministers, the People's Alliance. The group became the main opposition party for much of the 1980s and as party leader, Fraga remained at the forefront of national politics. In 1990 he became regional president of his native Galicia, where he won four successive elections, before he was finally ousted in 2005. Unwilling to step away from public office, even at the age of 82, Fraga served as a national senator for a further six years. He wasn't the retiring type.

***

Cycling along the shore, I noticed a sign for Mojácar, which bore the words 'One of Spain's most beautiful towns' written in English. The previous evening, Benito had been extremely inquisitive about my route (which had, of course, fed into my paranoia) and suggested I took time to explore Mojácar. Now that I had established he wasn't an axe murderer (sorry for doubting you, Benito), I decided to follow his advice.

The high regard the town is now held in represents quite a turnaround. As recently as 1960, Mojácar didn't have running water, electricity or telephone lines. Step forward another enterprising mayor: Jacinto Alarcón. Prior to his appointment in 1960, Mojácar's population had fallen from 6,000 people to just 600 within four decades. To reverse this trend, Alarcón gave away land to individuals prepared to restore old houses or build new ones. The town promptly began to attract intellectuals, artists and journalists and word began to spread of its beauty. The buildings were painted white and, thanks to Alarcón's ability to gain friends in high places, such as Manuel Fraga, Mojácar was awarded the national 'El Pueblo Blanco' prize in 1964.

From the beach I could see the old town's whitewashed buildings nestled in the distant foothills of the Sierra Cabrera mountain range. I was drenched in sweat by the time I made it to the old town, and ultimately, it probably wasn't worth the effort. I should have realised it before, but there isn't much to do in an old town other than to wander through the admittedly pretty cobbled streets. I preferred the charms of Altea's old town. Mojácar took a little too much satisfaction in its own celebrated status. It was like the village of

Sandford in the film *Hot Fuzz*, minus the grizzly murders. Or maybe I just got lucky.

I returned to the coast and cycled along an idyllic stretch of road that connected various seaside towns. Following a long climb inland, I neared the tiny hillside village of Sopalmo. If I hadn't already committed to staying in Almería that night, I would have happily luxuriated over a lazy lunch at one of the tempting family-run roadside restaurants. Instead, I continued across a bridge spanning a 10-metre wide bone dry riverbed that was difficult to imagine as a flowing waterway. The road snaked ever higher through the mountains until it reached the Granatilla lookout.

The descent back towards the sea was straight out of a car advert. The sea sparkled in the sunlight as the road zigzagged down the mountain. I passed a predictably redundant 30-metre wide river mouth before using the last of my energy to climb the rolling hills outside Carboneras. As at El Campello, I was hungry when I arrived at the seaside resort and rectified this by gorging myself on carbohydrates bought from a local bakery while I sat on the beach.

It wasn't long before I was heading back uphill. Just as I was beginning to rue my gluttony, I noticed several cars congregating by the roadside. Intrigued, I jumped off my bike and joined the drivers admiring the view of Playa de los Muertos far below. The beach gained its tragic sobriquet due to the frequency with which the bodies of shipwrecked sailors were found on the shore. I subsequently learned that the spot had been named Spain's best beach by a popular website in each of the three previous years. In all honesty, it didn't *seem* much better than many of the other stretches of sand that I'd passed. I would have loved to have been able to deliver a definitive verdict, but the sun's intensity was already abating, so I carried on.

By this stage, my chances of arriving in time for the football appeared slim. Thankfully, over the next 40km the gentle hills descended almost imperceptibly towards Almería and I made good progress as I listened to podcasts on the wondrously empty open roads.

As I got closer to the city, enormous tented farms stretched across the landscape. The dusty structures of tape and opaque, flimsy plastic gave them a ramshackle appearance, but by looking through occasional tears in the material I could see there was nothing makeshift about them. Inside, sophisticated technology had been installed to guarantee high yields. Agriculture has grown exponentially over the last 50 years to play an important role in Almería's resurgence. The tents now cover more than 6,000 hectares, forming the largest concentration of greenhouses in the world and producing half of Europe's fruit and vegetables inside them. Considering the region receives less than 2cm of rainfall on average each month, this is a remarkable feat.

When bricks and mortar began to replace the polythene tents, I turned onto a small coastal road that ran parallel to the city's airport. I thought this might make a pleasant change to passing out-of-town retail parks, but I soon regretted the decision. The road was predictably flat, but the strong crosswinds whipped up by the sea to my left made it feel like I was cycling through treacle. My desire to arrive in time to see the football turned this final leg of the journey into a race against the clock. There weren't any planes taking off or landing, so I had nothing else to distract me from the seemingly never-ending airport perimeter fence at my side.

Having put the runway behind me at last, I cycled the final couple of kilometres along the seafront, with the beach on one flank and tall palm trees on the other. Together they created a pleasing funnel, reminiscent of well-wishers at the end of a long race.

Thanks to Real Madrid's participation in the final, it wasn't difficult to find a bar showing the game. Some fans were inside marquees, but many others were sitting around screens outside. It showed that even the locals believed summer was on its way. I ordered a beer and pulled up a plastic seat just as the players were coming out of the tunnel.

The match will go down in history as the end of goalkeeper Loris Karius' Liverpool career. He calamitously let in Real Madrid's first goal and was at least partly to blame for their third. Liverpool later claimed he had been concussed. As the Madrid fans celebrated at the final whistle, it was hard not to feel sympathy for the player as tears rolled down his face.

14

Almería

In Almería I stayed with Connor, a quiet young Irishman living in a small flat with a mysterious girlfriend who I heard but never saw. After covering 234km in 48 hours and the high stress, however ill-founded, of the nocturnal adventure in Vera, I was happy to take it easy for a couple of days. Which was just as well. My first day in Almería was a Sunday and almost everything was closed, so I ambled through the public squares before spending the rest of the day sprawled on the beach.

The city was revitalised by the start of the working week and nowhere was this more true than in Almería's huge indoor food market. The owners of stalls on the ground floor were selling a mesmerising variety of colourful fruit and vegetables. In addition, there were several butchers, each hanging hefty joints of cured ham above shiny glass display counters. The escalator down into the basement revealed a large supermarket, presumably serving customers who didn't wish to support local businesses.

Bright morning sunlight bathed the square next to the market and after eating breakfast I visited the city's cathedral. As was the case in Vera, the building had impregnable walls to defend it from pirate raids. Similarly, the city's most famous attraction, the Alcazaba, was also designed to keep people out. The word alcazaba originates from the Arabic *al-qasbah* and describes a walled fortification in a city. The landmark was shut when I visited, but as I made my way there I was surprised to see a statue of John Lennon in a small, forgotten square. It marked the Beatles' time in Almería in 1966, during which they wrote *Strawberry Fields Forever*.

The alcazaba has three defensive walls and, looking up at the ramparts, I didn't fancy my chances of breaching them. Its formidable appearance has made the site popular with film studios and it most recently featured in *Wonder Woman 1984*. Many films have also been shot at Fort Bravo in the Tabernas Desert, just north of the city. This little-known film village was specially built in the 1950s to resemble the American Wild West. Considering the set's distance from Hollywood, it sounds counterintuitive, but production costs were often cheaper here and the location provided better accessibility to the open vistas desired by directors than other, more remote places.

Lawrence of Arabia (1962), *Once Upon a Time in the West*

(1968) and *Indiana Jones and the Last Crusade* (1989) were all filmed in the Tabernas Desert. So too were parts of *Game of Thrones*, although I'm yet to visit a destination which doesn't lay claim to being the location of at least a few scenes from the series. Almería's tourist industry is less forthcoming about its role in cinematic flops, which include 2004's *Lucky Luke and the Daltons* (which boasts an impressively low rating on IMDB of 3.2) and 2014's widely derided *Ridley Scott epic Exodus: Gods and Kings.*

I walked down from the alcazaba through the tightly packed streets of the medina to rejoin the holidaymakers on the beach soaking up the sunshine. The next few days would almost certainly be the toughest of the trip so far and I set about carefully plotting my route. From the moment I'd conceived of the ride, I had been eager to visit Granada. Geographically, this made no sense at all as it necessitated cycling more than 200km inland to then return straight back to the coast near Malaga. Nevertheless, everyone I knew who had been to Granada had waxed lyrical about the city and I knew I'd rue any decision to omit it from my itinerary. The only complication was the small issue of needing to cross the daunting Sierra Nevada to get there.

15

Almería to Beires

The initial section of the journey north was a gradual ascent, but as the sun began to rise in the sky, the hills either side of the road rose too. I made unexpectedly good progress and estimated I might arrive in Beires in time for a late lunch. The village is located just shy of 1km above sea level and I was looking forward to spending the afternoon gazing at the increasingly spectacular views, instead of looking down at the frame of my bike as I strained to reach one summit after another.

The section of the journey to Canjáyar sticks out in my mind not only because of its severity, but because of its cruelty to the psychology of anyone foolish enough to cycle it. At the bottom of the incline, a road sign informed drivers that the 70km/h speed limit was over -

just as it became tricky for me to exceed a tenth of that.

From this point I could see Canjáyar's traditional white cubic buildings further up the mountainside. Not exactly close, but near enough so that they represented something to aim towards. The deception of the topography was revealed during the ascent though, for the road first climbed high above the village and swung around the back of it, like a hawk stalking an unsuspecting field mouse. Even the engines of the few vehicles on the road began to splutter indignantly as the slope intensified.

I barely thought about it at the time - I struggled to think of anything other than the effort required to keep pedalling - but I undoubtedly benefitted from the road's recent resurfacing. Unlike many of the pot-holed roads I had come across, the tarmac here was in perfect condition and laid out like a Scalextric track. A long hill straight led to a masterly engineered 180° turn around a bend that was built atop of a viaduct 400 metres in length. As I struggled towards it, the ebullience of the cyclist who passed me going the other way was etched across his face. My private envy only subsided upon reaching the viaduct, when I too was able to admire the incredible views back across the sunlight hills of the Sierra de Gádor.

From afar, the road beyond the viaduct had appeared less severe. Perhaps it marginally was. But it certainly didn't feel any easier. My legs felt empty from the climb and the ferocious power of the sun beating down on the back of my neck had sapped my energy. When I finally arrived at one of the many viewpoints at Canjáyar, I fought to catch my breath while admiring the surrounding valleys. I smiled ruefully at the memory of a description I'd read of the village's location 'at the foot of the Sierra Nevada'.

Inevitably, villages were becoming increasingly sporadic as I cycled deeper into the mountains. After half an hour I pulled in at the next one along - a small settlement called Almócita. As it was barely more than a kilometre short of Beires, many would argue I could, and should, have pushed on. However, the villages were also separated by 100 metres of elevation, so I paused for what turned out to be one of my favourite lunches of the trip.

I had stumbled upon a beautiful village with a quaint square dominated by an ornamental water fountain, whose trickling water provided the only accompaniment to the sound of crickets buzzing in the nearby hills. Curiously, I didn't see a single one of Almócita's 150 residents as I walked through the empty cobbled streets. Just as I was about to give up on hopes of finding a place to eat, I ventured around a corner to find a few individuals gathered in the shade under some trees next to what I strongly suspected was the village's sole restaurant. My arrival turned heads.

'*¿Desde dónde ha pedaleado?*' asked one of the elderly men as he looked at my bike. Where have you come from?

'*Monté mi bici desde Almería esta mañana,*' I replied, enjoying the visible disbelief in their reaction.

There were no sandwiches on the menu, so I broke the bank and opted for the cheapest *ración* on offer: *morcilla* and chips. While I waited for it to be cooked, I watched my fellow diners on the neighbouring tables. Relaxing in the shade, they consumed their food and drink so slowly, it was as if it was completely incidental as to why they were sat there. When my own lunch was served, I should have followed suit, but I lacked the necessary restraint.

I'd never tried *morcilla* before. My initial wariness of its dark, shrunken and phallic ugliness was instantly swept away by the joy of eating it, as it was, without doubt, one of the most flavoursome sausages I'd ever had. I vowed to find somewhere that served this exotic speciality in the UK and messaged my friends back home to tell them of my discovery. So I was disappointed, and more than a little embarrassed, when I found out online that this foreign delicacy was merely a local variant of black pudding. Almost exactly the same as the black pudding I had always gone out of my way to avoid because I didn't like the idea of eating dried blood.

Re-energised and full of iron, I began the final stretch towards Beires. The village was even smaller than Almócita, but I still found it difficult to find where I was staying as many of the steep streets were too small to feature on the map. The only person I saw was a plump woman outside a building near to where I believed my accommodation to be, but whose blank expression led me to assume I was mistaken.

I always told my prospective hosts I was coming by bike and when I arrived, several said they had recognised me from afar. Not so in Beires. Even though I clearly wasn't a local (my host would surely have known me personally if I was), and in spite of that fact that I had accurately informed her of both the manner and approximate time of my arrival, it appeared my host hadn't contemplated the possibility she may be the person I was looking for. After pushing my laden bike in circles a few more times around the neighbourhood, I returned to the building and tentatively introduced myself to the woman. She was officious, curt and not at all pleased to see me.

As you might anticipate, in remote mountain villages such as this there were not a plethora of places to stay. Unlike the spare bedrooms in flats that I had become accustomed to, my room in Beires was, I found to my surprise, part of a small hotel. It was my bad luck that the owners didn't regard customers from Airbnb as bona fide guests.

The woman I spoke to was highly sceptical my booking existed and treated me with the disdain of a salesman selling a Ponzi scheme. She shut the front door on me as she went inside to verify my reservation, before opening it again and showing me to my room with barely concealed resentment. The room wasn't as nice as the one advertised, but by this point I thought better of mentioning it.

This was far from the warm welcome I had hoped to receive. Having already explored every corner of the village looking for my accommodation, I sat on a park bench by the parish church, marvelling at the breathtaking view over the valley. The sun illuminated the surrounding peaks and the cluster of properties below that formed Almócita. As I watched the sun move slowly move across the sky, I called Sarah. She was on a stressful journey to a wedding in the outer reaches of Scotland. I'd been invited, and had briefly thought about attending, but I barely knew the couple and instinctively knew I much preferred being in Beires. Even if I did have to tolerate a bad-tempered hotel owner.

I would have chosen somewhere, anywhere, other than

the hotel to eat dinner, but nowhere was open. This was perhaps to be expected as I could count on one hand the number of people I had seen since I'd arrived in Beires. It felt a world away from Almería, yet I appreciated the isolation. I hadn't cycled into the mountains to have the same experience that I'd had along the coast. Here there was no danger I'd be targeted by overzealous market traders looking to flog fake sunglasses.

Still, it was a little unsettling to be the only guest in the dining room at dinner. There is something undeniably sad about seeing a local hotel palpably struggle to survive. The current prevalence of aggregator websites has forced hotels to pay high levels of commission in order to be listed, greatly eroding their already paper-thin margins. However, the behaviour of the staff made it hard to feel sympathetic.

Hostilities were renewed when the owners kept changing the cost of the various components of the meal. It became evident they wanted me to pay as high a price as possible to eat as many microwaved oddments as they could find in the back of the cupboards. I'd like to say it was a meal that wouldn't stay long in the memory, but on a trip where interaction with others was often at a premium, my recollection of the meal and the strained discourse around it, remains vivid.

Ah well. Almócita, you will always have a place in my heart.

16

Beires to Guadix

I didn't stay long the following morning. My request to be offered the breakfast included in my original booking was met with rancour, and once I'd eaten a bit of cold toast, an apple and a muffin tasting of cardboard, I left in haste.

Due to the paucity of accommodation in the Sierra Nevada, I had taken a detour to reach Beires. Ideally, I would have turned right off the main road before Canjayar, saving myself from the 11km uphill slog to Beires. This would have negated the need to cycle the same distance again to get to Ohanes, which on paper is barely 3km due north of Canjayar. But I knew finding a place to spend the night was imperative. Even in summer it isn't a good idea to sleep under the Sierra Nevada stars wearing just a thin jumper.

While sleeping in the wild would have saved me the misfortune of meeting my host in Beires, I would also have missed out on one of the most memorable parts of the trip. I set off into the cool morning full of vigour and glad to be out on my own in the fresh, clean air as the sun crept gradually over the mountains towering around me. The few vehicles on the road were all old, noisy, worn-down trucks driven by local farmers. Except for them, the only sound was the occasional whistling of the wind. The silence ensured that while I may not have been able to see the rusty vehicles coming around the blind corners, I could hear the approach of their throaty engines in time to take the necessary evasive action to avoid falling from the unprotected precipices.

As I ascended, I admired the views and the mixture of poppies and bright yellow flowers that had sprung up in the gravel by the roadside. Just before 9am I turned a bend in the road that revealed the village of Ohanes on the hill opposite. Ohanes' population size is more than three times larger than Almócita and Beires combined. The unexpected sight of its buildings clinging to the hillside made me recall a famous photograph I had seen years before of the Potala Palace in the Tibetan capital of Lhasa. For centuries it served as the winter palace of the Dalai Lama. Like Ohanes, the monumental structure is predominantly white, is built on a hill and has a stone centrepiece. But while the palace's centrepiece resembles a fort, Ohanes' focal point is a church. The sun had not yet reached the village when I arrived and at this time in the morning it was too cold to stay still in the shade for long, so after eating an orange I got back on the bike and resumed climbing.

To my surprise, the road plateaued for about a kilometre as I neared Tices, the next settlement along. I paused to look back in the direction from whence I had come and was gratified to see Almería in the distance. The Sierra Nevada, whose name translates as the 'Snowy Mountains', is one of the few places in Europe where you can ski within sight of the sea. Having been taken aback by the size of Ohanes, I'd anticipated Tices to be much larger than it was, but it consisted merely of a few buildings constructed around a cute terracotta coloured church, whose beauty surely surpassed its utility.

Just beyond the church there was a small downhill. For the first time, I dared to imagine that the most challenging section of my journey over the Sierra Nevada was behind me.

The folly of that train of thought was exposed almost immediately. The gruelling hill that followed laid bare my mental fragility as self-doubt and self-loathing echoed inside my head. What kind of idiot was I to believe I could cycle across the Sierra Nevada on a £150 bike while carrying more weight on my panniers than most drivers have in their car boot? This wasn't just daft, this was reckless.

One of my main difficulties was the fundamental issue that the lowest gear on a cheap bike isn't really all that low. As a rule, more expensive bikes have more gears, and certainly more high-quality components. If you buy a decent new bike today, it's likely to have at least 18 gears as standard. Mine had only seven. Try as I might, I just couldn't get the cadence up to establish the forward momentum I needed to stay upright on the steep incline. This meant that to save myself from keeling over sideways like a child learning to ride a bike, I had to stop regularly. Each time I did, I sipped water in an attempt to replace the sweat that was pouring down my face in the rapidly intensifying heat. On such a climb there's no shame in that - except for that fact that each time I did this, the distance I travelled between each break shortened. Soon I was barely moving 10 metres before having to pause again. Eventually I accepted defeat and walked a couple of hundred metres before the burning pride of my bruised ego got me back in the saddle.

To lift my spirits, I started playing music from my phone. And so it was, singing Billy Joel's *She's Always a Woman*, in time not to the music but to the slow, painful revolutions of my pedals, that I at last reached the summit. At more than 1,300 metres altitude, I was at the highest point of my journey across the Sierra Nevada. I had made it.

My route had taken me over the eastern part of the mountain range. Back in Almería, I had been disappointed to have to abort plans to cycle via the ski resort of Puerto de la Ragua due to the lack of accommodation available nearby in summer. That route would have required me to climb an additional 700 metres of altitude. As much as I love a challenge, as I sat panting by the edge of the road, I regarded it not as a missed opportunity, but as a lucky escape. Approximately 50km to the west lay Mount Mulhacén. Standing at 3,482 metres above sea level, it is the highest point on the Spanish mainland. That was one I definitely wanted to avoid.

Almost before I knew it, I was heading downhill towards Abla. On a trip with several incredible downhill stretches, this was quite possibly the best of the lot. The road was clear and I relished negotiating the countless hairy hairpin bends. Long after the initial excitement had subsided, the road kept on going and going, snaking out of view deep into the valley below.

I knew the effort-intensive hours of peddling that morning hadn't made much of a dent on the total distance I needed to cycle to reach Guadix and I had begun to wonder how late it would be by the time I arrived. So this seemingly endless descent was just what I needed. The road finally levelled out at the end of an exhilarating 400-metre drop in altitude.

Abla is a completely unremarkable roadside town, but people come from miles around to visit. Why? Because it has a supermarket, which, as a consequence of its rarity, was a hive of activity. As I feasted my hungry eyes on the stacked shelves, I noticed everyone around me was shouting at each other like stock market traders desperate to clinch a deal. A man was bellowing in the direction of a woman at the till, while she was animatedly pointing at a shop assistant in the aisle, who herself was having a fraught conversation with another customer. Disappointingly, with so many 'conversations' occurring simultaneously, I couldn't quite work out what was being said. Perhaps they were all as famished as I was.

Once I'd bought some food, I walked, bewildered, out of the shop. There was nowhere to sit down, so I leaned against the parked trolleys and tore into the fresh bread. I hadn't given much thought as to what the terrain would be like on the other side of the Sierra Nevada and I was curious as to what lay ahead after such a spectacular start to the day.

The answer was one of the least exciting stretches of road of the whole trip. For the first time since I left Valencia, clouds filled the sky and while they didn't ever threaten to release rain, their thick grey blanket reflected the relative mundanity of the cycle.

I travelled along small, empty dirt tracks and minor roads for the next few hours. The flat topography may have been uninspiring but it was certainly easier on my legs and, in the absence of traffic, I whiled away the miles occasionally spotting some of the Sierra Nevada's snow-capped peaks through breaks in the cloud.

As I ground out the miles towards Guadix, I was astonished to see a fort on the horizon. Its location atop of a small hill created a stark outline against the dark afternoon sky. Intrigued, I took a detour to gain a better view. If the church at Tices a few hours before had looked out of place, Calahorra Castle was completely at odds with its surroundings. It had a domed turret at each corner of the fort, giving it the appearance of something belonging to the dunes of Tatooine in *Star Wars*. The castle is now largely forgotten, but when it was built in the early 16th century, it was one of the first Italian Renaissance castles to be built outside of Italy.

I rejoined the road heading west and stopped at Alcudia de Guadix. Just 7km from the city of Guadix, I'd imagined this pit-stop to be an uninteresting suburb, but it has a beautiful church and a separate chapel built on a small hill above the town. Even on an overcast day such as this, I could see Calahorra Castle to the south-east and Guadix further along the road to the north-west. Directly opposite, the mountains of the Sierra Nevada reared up, and although the clouds were too low to see the very top, the snow line was visible.

I cycled back down through the town's narrow streets and began the day's final push. Guadix was by far the largest place I had come across since leaving Almería, with a population of nearly 20,000 people. Its grand Baroque cathedral would not have looked out of place in Madrid or Barcelona and the Spanish flag draped over a balcony high up the tower lent the building an air of regality. Unfortunately, the landmark has been somewhat undermined by the massive hole next to it. In 2007 the construction of a car park uncovered Roman ruins and now an excavation site more than 100 metres long and 50 metres wide has been sealed off from public use. Barring a truly remarkable discovery, it seems a shame that such a vast space in the very centre of the city has been assigned to remember events that took place two millennia ago. But maybe that's just the prejudiced sentiment of someone more interested in modern history.

After exploring more of Guadix, I met my host, Mateo, in his flat on the outskirts of the city. A diminutive man in his early thirties, he was so quiet I was never sure whether he was in the flat or not. In the silence, I became aware of the noise my presence generated, so I went out to eat some tapas from a restaurant around the corner. The only other customers were a group of local men drinking heavily. I pretended not to notice the inquisitive looks they cast my way when I arrived. They soon lost interest and began shouting indiscernibly at the news being shown on a small television mounted on the wall.

I ordered what I hoped would be the most filling tapas I could find - a selection of bread, ham, *morcilla* (of course) and an unspecified type of fish slathered in mayonnaise. But it barely touched the sides. I sloped off, leaving the men to their beers and headed hungrily into the Lidl next door. The sky was no longer overcast and the sunlight hit the remaining fragments of cloud, turning them a fierce pink. I ate a couple of pastries as I sat contentedly in the supermarket car park, watching the sky slowly turn crimson.

17

Guadix to Granada

The following morning, the clouds had disappeared altogether and the sun shone brightly in the clear blue sky. The old wives' tale had held true; the shepherds would have been delighted. Although my route to Granada took me around the back of the Sierra Nevada, and thus avoided the biggest climbs, I knew plenty of steep ascents lay ahead. But before I could make the most of the moderate temperature of the crisp early morning air, I first went to explore Guadix's biggest, and most unusual, claim to fame.

It takes something special to upstage such a magnificent cathedral, but Guadix is also home to a unique district called the Neighbourhood of Caves. Upon arrival, the sight of white chimneys sticking up above the grassy mounds felt deeply surreal, like I'd come across a Hollywood movie set that had been abandoned before it could be dismantled. Yet this is far from a quaint regional quirk. There are more than 2,000 underground dwellings in active use, some of which date back a millennium. Collectively, they make up the largest number of cave homes anywhere in Europe. The caves provide natural protection from the blistering heat of the summer sun and insulate inhabitants in winter from the chilling winds that whip off the Sierra Nevada.

In total more than 6,000 people, known as troglodytes, still live in the caves. Traditionally, the caves were home to the poorer members of Guadix's population. While the city's wealthier residents appreciated the novelty of the dwellings, many looked down upon those who actually lived in them. However, in recent years, the caves have gained a certain cache, and as a result, have become much more desirable places to live. Indeed, many of these homes now have all the mod cons one could desire: internet access, dishwashers, marble floors et al. Some even have swimming pools.

Admittedly, it hadn't reached 8am yet, but the pace of life here felt perceptibly slower. The few residents I saw all wished me good morning as they went about their morning chores. I walked up a small footpath that encircled one of the nearby mounds like a helter skelter. From the top, I was able to comprehend the scale of the neighbourhood for the first time. The dazzling sunlight made it uncomfortable to take in all of the white walls and chimneys, so I looked instead towards the city centre, where I could see the cathedral in the distance.

Guadix's metropolitan centre felt a hundred miles

away from the chimneys that poked out of the mounds and the jagged ochre terrain around me. In reality the distance was barely 650 metres. Refocusing my gaze on the caves, I noticed smoke emerging from a chimney poking out of a nearby mound. It must be strange having people walk on your roof at all times of the day. No doubt an estate agent would have marketed the cave as a bungalow with period features and a rooftop terrace.

Walking slowly around the district, I studied the dwellings carefully. Each is built into a different section of a hill and each, as a consequence, has a unique appearance. While some have obscured entrances, many others have front rooms and porches that extend outwards from the original structure.

I reluctantly pulled myself away from the enchanting caves to make inroads into the day's cycle. At least that was the plan. I had only travelled a few kilometres when I reached Purullena and noticed an 'open' sign pointing to a roadside cave museum. It was a two-storey building in front of a hill whose pronounced apex rose 15 metres above the pavement. My curiosity piqued, both by the museum's contents and its uncommonly early opening time, I pulled up outside.

I was aware of the heavy price the sun would make me pay later in the day if I lingered for long, but before I could take a closer look at the museum, a middle-aged man with a scraggly beard and balding scalp walked out of the building towards me.

If he had given me the hard sell, I would have been on my heels, but he said genially, '*La entrada cuesta 2€ y puedes hacer fotos*'. It's €2 to come in and you're welcome to take photos.

As he watched me mull it over, he added, '*Mi familia es dueña de la cueva desde hace 140 años. Todavía vivo en una parte de ella y el interior se mantiene igual a cuando estaban vivos mis padres*'. My family have owned this cave for 140 years. I still live in part of it and I've kept the inside the same as when my parents were alive.

This clinched it for me. Without a clue of what the cave's interior would look like, I walked into the man's home, hoping he wasn't Spain's answer to Norman Bates. I had anticipated that he'd want to give me a guided tour, but he remained outside. At the time I was impressed by how trusting he was of visitors, but it was just as likely that he knew there wasn't anything inside worth taking.

The cave had painted domed ceilings and open-plan rooms, which were separated by curtains rather than doors. The domed ceilings ensure the weight of the soil is distributed towards the outer side of the walls, while the open-plan layout allows air to circulate through the cave more effectively. I only learned all this much later and was unaware of either benefit as I walked through the house, as it didn't include any information points. This made it feel much less like a museum, and more like I had turned up unannounced and strode directly into someone's living room. Which, in many ways, I had.

Although the owner was happy for me to take photographs, I felt uneasy about using my camera. Regardless of the intent, it felt rude to start taking photos of his home as if I was on a trip to the zoo. The rooms would have felt more homely, and the experience perhaps less peculiar, were it not for the fact that practically every inch of the walls was covered by an array of ornaments so bizarre and antiquated that even a charity shop would turn its nose up at them. These included a mixture of pots and pans, ceramics and a variety of obsolete farming equipment. I couldn't tell who this eclectic decor was for. Was it on display for the benefit of visitors? Or because the owner's parents had thought it brought extra character to the place?

I had expected the cave to consist of just a few rooms dug into the hill, but as I explored one room after another, I appreciated for the first time how deceptively large some cave dwellings must be. This cave had three floors and I swiftly lost my bearings in relation to the outside world. It felt like I was in a Tardis. A cold Tardis at that, for the cave's natural insulation kept the air noticeably cooler than it was outside. While this benefits cave dwellers in the height of summer, it made the cave, and its hanging trinkets, feel eerie as I walked between its cold stone walls. If anything was to happen to me while alone in the depths of this man's cave house, I was sure I wouldn't be found until I was a skeleton in a rocking chair.

As I walked up another set of stairs, a rare sign pointed me towards drawn curtains where shards of natural light shone through gaps separating the draped sheets. I pulled the material back and walked out into the blindingly bright sunlight that bathed the balcony and the street it overlooked below. Enjoying the sun's warmth, I looked out over other neighbouring cave dwellings and further afield to the snowy mountaintops of the Sierra Nevada. I then retraced my steps to the cave's entrance, thanking the man for his hospitality as I left. It was now nearly 10am. I was nowhere near where I had hoped to be by this time of the day, but I'd had all the more memorable morning as a result of my spontaneous tour.

Shortly after passing the town of Los Baños, the road began a gradual incline towards an ominous mountain in the distance. I can't be sure, but it may well have been the mighty Mulhacén. Thankfully, the road soon bore right and away from the peak, saving me from climbing its surrounding foothills. My route promptly took on a very different feel. The road had been cut through the mountainside and sheer red rock towered several metres either side of it, obscuring my view of what lay around each corner.

Gradually, the road opened up, taking me on a meandering course through the countryside towards La Peza. Snowmelt and regional rainfall makes the environment here noticeably more verdant than much of the sparse land I travelled through elsewhere. From La Peza the route began to ascend, starting gradually and rising in intensity as the altitude increased.

The road, like so many others in Spain, had posts demarcating each kilometre. These indicated how far along the road you were at that particular point. On hills such as this, where I needed to travel many kilometres along the same road, these marker posts irrefutably showed how painfully slowly I was moving. The distances between the posts seemed to grow exponentially as the incline increased. At times like these I hated the markers. But the only thing worse than seeing them, was not, and the intervals between each became a purgatory of burning lactic acid.

Just after 1.30pm, I inched towards a brown sign that read: 'Puerto de los Blancares 1,297m'. Translated literally, the name means 'Door to the Whites', a hint that, at other times of the year, I would be cycling through a blanket of snow. Tired though I was, it seemed a shame to fall just short of 1,300 metres. Alpine trees bordered the road, but I resisted the temptation to clamber up a nearby trunk to gain the extra 3m. Instead, I rewarded myself with a handful of almonds. About a minute later, two wiry women in their fifties cycled towards me from the opposite direction.

I gave them a cursory glance. They weren't carrying much and while their bikes were superior to mine, they weren't top of the range. Furthermore, although they were breathing hard as they reached the summit, they looked far less exhausted than I felt. From these brief observations, I concluded the descent that lay ahead must be less steep than the one I'd just completed.

To my surprise, the two women seemed excited to see me. I gathered myself for this unexpected opportunity to practise my Spanish. But they could spot a fellow tourist from a mile off and interrupted my efforts to make small talk in the language. Instead, they peppered me with questions in English, with each new query coming before I could answer the previous one.

'Where have you come from?'

'How did you get here?'

'Where did you cross over the mountains?'

Disguising my disappointment, I talked them through my route over the past couple of days. I tried to downplay it, but inside I was proud of what I had achieved. Yet the women in front of me were underwhelmed.

'We're going to cycle over Puerto de la Ragua. We plan to do it today, but if not we'll take it on tomorrow.'

I tried to hide my scepticism. They had many miles to go and hundreds of metres to climb that afternoon. Moreover, it wasn't clear how they intended to find accommodation. At any rate, they were convinced they would succeed, so I wished them luck as they headed down the hill I'd just cycled up. As they disappeared from view, my pride turned to a nagging sense of self-doubt. Had I taken the easy route over the Sierra Nevada? Would I regret my decision? Reflecting upon the pain I'd been in just five minutes earlier, I reminded myself there was nothing easy about cycling over these mountains and any sense of regret vanished instantly.

The cycle down from the peak was superb. It wasn't terrifyingly steep, but more than sufficient to make my eyes stream as the trees flew past and the road curved its way down towards the valley. It may not have been quite as challenging as my approach from the other side, but it certainly would have been hard work. I had a newfound respect for the intrepid travellers I'd just met. Perhaps they would make it to Puerto de la Ragua after all.

Even as I descended I could feel the fatigue in my legs and I promised myself I would stop for lunch at the bottom of the hill. My habit of only allowing myself to stop when I'd reached a certain milestone often caused me to eschew perfectly pleasant places for a picnic in the hope there would be something equally agreeable at my own self-imposed checkpoint. This wasn't always the case, so I'd often end up eating lunch by busy roadsides or in areas of long grass. I invariably received puzzled looks from local cyclists and motorists, who can only have assumed I was lost.

Fortunately, on this occasion luck was with me. While

I did engender plenty of attention from passersby, this time they were from people looking at me not with bewilderment, but with envy. From the dusty roadside bend where I finally ran out of momentum, the view was so beautiful, several motorists parked up next to me to take photographs. An impossibly picturesque swathe of emerald green water cut through the surrounding hills, reminiscent of Patagonia in Chile. In some respects, it was too good to be true. The landscape was at least partially man-made for it had been shaped by the creation of Quéntar Reservoir, one of the principal water sources for the 200,000 people living in Granada.

After lunch I carried on cycling along the road, parallel to the water until I approached the dam. At this point, the road curved away from the water's edge and I began the long descent that continued almost all the way to Granada. At lunch I had once again been mildly concerned about the many kilometres I still had to travel that day, but the distance melted away, aided immeasurably by the fact that, for much of it, I barely needed to peddle.

As I freewheeled downhill through groves of alpine trees, the views became more expansive and I was able to admire the majestic vista of the valley below. I felt sympathy for the cyclists coming towards me the other way. Their faces were either screwed up in torment at the effort required or hidden from view as they looked down at the asphalt beneath them. My cycle up to Puerto de los Blancares suddenly didn't seem so bad.

The road eventually plateaued just outside the village of Los Pinillos. From there, I followed the Genil river all the way to Granada. Initially, it was little more than a stream that ran through a glade of trees. However, as I approached the city, the river, swelled by tributaries, began to resemble a fast-flowing canal. It no longer meandered as before, with straight lines of stone levees directing the water towards the municipality. As I passed runners and young families on the paths either side of the river, I pictured myself playing a game of Pooh Sticks like I had as a child. I imagined myself throwing a large twig into the river back in Los Pinillos and following its course on my bike as it floated the remaining 7km towards the city centre.

I was deep in thought about the type of stick I'd choose for such a game when I came to the end of a large shady park. A couple of hundred metres away, I could see heavy traffic flowing over a stone bridge supported by five arches. Wondering where I was, I studied the map and realised I'd reached Plaza del Humilladero. I had arrived in Granada.

I ambled through the park, past amorous couples sitting on black metal benches, as I walked towards the heart of the city. Adjoining the park is the popular promenade of Carrera de la Virgen where artisans displayed paintings and small wooden crafts for sale. Dodging my way through the crowds (not an easy thing to do with a bike carrying stuffed pannier bags), I made my way to the large water fountain in Plaza del Campillo. The square is one of the city's major meeting points and in the afternoon sun it was teeming with happy residents and tourists. Many were gathered under the sporadically planted trees, seeking shelter from the little shade they provided. Ever the Englishman abroad, I did the opposite and, after locking my bike, enjoyed eating an ice cream in the sunshine.

Next to the Plaza del Campillo is the Plaza de Mariana Pineda. Today it plays host to several cafes and cocktail bars, but it used to be an execution site and takes its present name from a liberalist heroine who was killed here in 1831.

During the dictatorial reign of Fernando VII, Mariana was charged with conspiracy after a flag was found at her home promoting 'Equality, Freedom and Law'. The incriminating flag was burned in front of her at her execution. If this punishment seems disproportionately harsh, it says much about Fernando VII's character. Widely regarded as a terrible monarch, historian Stanley Payne describes him as 'cowardly, selfish, grasping, suspicious, and vengeful', which sound like the names of five of the less popular dwarfs. By contrast, Mariana Pineda's courage is still heralded today. Her story has been depicted numerous times and she was famously portrayed on television by former Altea resident, and General Franco favourite, Pepa 'Marisol' Flores.

Predictably, trying to find a cheap place to stay in Granada had been tricky. I ended up reserving a room in a flat far away on the other side of the city. The listing said I would be hosted by Lorenzo, but, after some confusion, I was met instead by his mother. After checking out the room, I asked if I could stay an extra night. But I was too late - someone had already snapped it up - so I would need to find somewhere else to stay the following evening. Resolving to address that problem the next day, I dropped my bags off and then, because of the distance, cycled back to the cobbled streets and little alleyways of the city centre. It didn't matter how tired I was, I always felt as light as a feather and free as a bird once I'd removed my laden pannier bags from my bike.

***

Upon arriving in Granada in 1350, Abu Abdullah Muhammad Ibn Battuta was deeply impressed and described the city as the 'metropolis of Andalucia [whose] environs have not their equal in any country in the world'. He would know; when it came to travelling, Ibn Battuta had been there, done that and got the T-shirt. Over the space of 30 years, he is said to have explored central Asia, south-east Asia, India, China, north Africa and southern Europe, amassing a total distance of around 117,000km. To put this into perspective, Marco Polo himself 'only' managed 12,000km.

Historians have queried the veracity of some of Ibn Battuta's accounts and his tales in China bear a suspiciously striking similarity to those recorded by Polo a few years before. From a purely logistical perspective, it would be a truly remarkable feat to marry and divorce as many women as he did (at least seven) while travelling on average almost 11km per day.

Nevertheless, even if he was prone to occasional exaggeration, Ibn Battuta was undoubtedly one of the medieval world's most well-travelled men. And as visitors to Granada have discovered for themselves ever since, the city has, often in spite of its inhabitants, retained much of the charm that captivated Ibn Battuta.

The history of Granada perfectly encapsulates the centuries of tension and conflict between the

Catholicism of the Spanish crown and the country's Muslim community. This period of history, known as the Reconquista, began in 711AD with the Umayyad conquest of Hispania, which saw almost the entirety of modern-day Spain and Portugal come under Muslim rule. Gradually eroded over time, this ended altogether nearly 800 years later when the last remaining Muslim dynasty on the Iberian Peninsula, the Nasrid kingdom in Granada, fell in 1492.

After a series of military campaigns, the last Muslim ruler, Emir Muhammad XII, signed the Alhambra Decree. Under the terms of the surrender, Muslims retained their freedom to practise their faith. The city's Jewish population meanwhile were expelled immediately.

Once in authority, the church ignored many of the conditions stipulated in the decree and the Islamic community was subjected to a targeted conversion campaign. This was originally led by the first archbishop of Granada, Hernando de Talavera. He believed Muslims would convert willingly to Christianity when they fully understood its virtues. His conviction led him to create the world's first bilingual Spanish-Arabic-Spanish dictionary.

The increasingly powerful Cardinal Francisco Jiménez de Cisneros grew frustrated with the slow pace of change though and at the turn of the century he replaced Talavera as archbishop. Cisneros regarded his predecessor's policies akin to 'giving pearls to pigs' and adopted a much more hardline approach. Supported by Queen Isabella, he prohibited the practice of Islam. In order to stay in the city, the majority of the Muslim community converted to Christianity, but they continued to be persecuted under their new status of Moriscos.

In the decades that followed, Arabic and Muslim clothing was banned and a Muslim rebellion lasting more than two years took place. By 1609 Spain was fighting wars in the Americas and was distracted by Turkish raids on its coastline. The monarchy had no patience for the recurring internal religious conflict and ordered the mass expulsion of Moriscos from the country. Hundreds of thousands of people were shipped off to north Africa, but many returned to Spain shortly afterwards by hopping on vessels travelling back across the Strait of Gibraltar. Other Moriscos remained in Spain simply by evading authorities. In the few places where the policy was implemented fully, such as in Valencia, the city's economy collapsed in the absence of the Morisco community.

While the expulsion policy had only limited success, the suppression of the original Muslim community during the 16th and 17th century changed the city's character irrevocably. In 1450 there had been 137 mosques in Granada, but just 50 years later, Cardinal Cisneros boasted 'all the mosques are churches', following a campaign that had seen the mosques converted into churches or simply destroyed. New structures replaced them, transforming the urban landscape. Yet in spite of the sustained effort to eliminate the city's Muslim heritage, Granada's popularity endures largely because of it.

The Alhambra is Granada's jewel in the crown and Spain's most visited tourist attraction. As such, it's a must-see destination, but its popularity comes at the cost of spontaneity and it's now also a must-book-ahead. I had reserved my ticket to visit the Islamic palace the next day, but I couldn't wait that long to catch a glimpse of the landmark. When people picture Granada, they often think of the famous view of the Alhambra atop of a green hilltop with the snow-covered mountains of the Sierra Nevada towering behind it. I'd seen this iconic image a hundred times, so I was keen to visit the viewpoint from where it was taken. I could have looked up the location online, but I decided it would have greater visual impact were I to simply stumble upon it. However, finding the vantage point turned out to be more difficult than I'd anticipated.

Arguably the city's busiest tourist spot is the area around Plaza Nueva (an unfortunate name considering it is now the city's oldest square) and the adjoining Plaza de Santa Ana. On one side is the River Darro, over the top of which the two plazas were built to create public space, and behind this, obscured by neighbouring buildings, is the steep hill on which the Alhambra sits. On the other side of the plazas is the UNESCO World Heritage Site of Albaicín. I knew the view I was looking for must be somewhere in Albaicín, but it's a deceptively large district spread across a hillside that is lined with narrow streets and tightly packed houses. Consequently, there wasn't an obvious place to see the Alhambra from, but rather several spots that warranted investigation.

After walking along the cobbled streets for some time, I found a public square directly opposite the Alhambra. Walking up and across the hillside for potential viewpoints had used the last of my energy and while it had been a fun challenge finding the lookout, I was relieved to have accomplished my mission.

Except I hadn't. While the square's elevated location provided a view of the Alhambra, it didn't, much to my disappointment, provide *the* view I sought. I expected to see some tourists milling around, but it was clear both Granada's tourism board and the city's authorities had turned a blind eye to the area. Approximately 15 men lay about across the square, variously drunk, high or just plain listless. They seemed as confused to see me as I was of them.

I hadn't felt this out of place since I went to Madrid as a 13-year-old with my mum. Early one afternoon we were walking along the main road through a park that had been endorsed by our out-of-date guide book, when the road became flanked by prostitutes. We walked on in bemused silence for a short while before my mum decided I'd seen more than enough and took the, in hindsight flawed, decision for us to divert off the main thoroughfare. Less than a minute had passed before a man suddenly popped up in the long grass 10 metres in front of us, pulling up his trousers and cursing incomprehensibly. A couple of seconds later, the woman he was with then stood up, looking much less flustered.

As I sat in the square in Granada, it felt like a long time since I had eaten lunch by the reservoir. My stomach was hankering for food, so I politely rebuffed offers to buy some weed and walked downhill to find something more substantial.

Conveniently, I found a restaurant offering a cheap pasta buffet. I would tell you the name, but I'm quite sure that after the amount I ate, they weren't in business for much longer. Midway through the meal 12 German

137

schoolgirls, all around 14 years old, arrived in the restaurant accompanied by their teacher. I couldn't help but eye them warily. As all regular buffet-goers know, it pays to be aware of the threat posed by your fellow diners. Some dare to have the temerity to consume all of your favourite dishes.

Having refilled my plate a couple of times, I noticed a few of the girls nudging each other as I returned to the buffet stand. I wanted to believe they were remarking on the strength of my tan, which by now had gained, if not quite a walnut shine, at least something akin to a dark amber. But in truth I suspected the girls were amused by how much I was consuming. I'm embarrassed to admit I was pleased the scope of my eating capacity impressed them, and I chided myself for thinking it was a shame they hadn't been in the restaurant to witness my performance from the start.

Sated, and having wowed a bunch of 14-year-old girls I'd never meet, I headed towards Granada's cathedral. Typically, the Spanish monarchy used the construction of the building to make a statement to the defeated Muslim population. The cathedral, like so many of the churches I visited in Spain, was built on top of a former mosque. It took nearly two centuries to complete and the construction time would have been far longer if the two 81-metre towers included in the original plans had been built.

By the time I arrived, the cathedral was closed so I walked around the base of the structure. Unlike in Guadix, where, as is common practice, the cathedral is given space to stand out and dominate its locality, in Granada buildings abut the cathedral on almost all sides.

During the day tourists, drawn to the cathedral like moths to a flame, walk in a slow procession through the bottleneck of neighbouring passageways. Once snared in the busy streets, they become sitting ducks for eager waiters and market vendors who stand, armed to the teeth with menus or locally made scarves, on either side of the alleyways.

This fate awaited me the next day. It was now 8.30pm though and, with the majority of tourists to be found elsewhere, the shops had closed. I wandered freely as I walked off some of my dinner and cycled back in the dark to my accommodation. When I arrived I tried to fit my bike vertically into the tiny lift up to the flat, but after twisting the bike into various positions, I was forced to admit defeat. Unwilling to risk leaving my bike out on the street overnight, I reluctantly began the slow process of carrying it up the four flights of stairs to the apartment.

18

Granada

Considering it's the gateway to the nation's most popular tourist attraction, the path up to the Alhambra isn't as clearly sign-posted as one would expect.

To allay my concerns that I was about to walk up a steep, tree-covered hill for no reason, I was looking at a map when a heavily accented Spanish voice asked in English, 'Is this the way to the Alhambra?'

I listened attentively for an answer, seeking confirmation from whoever the question had been directed at. It didn't come. Confused, I turned around to find the question had been directed at me. A handsome couple, a little older than myself, with dark brown hair and sun-kissed skin stood before me.

'I think it must be,' I offered, quite unhelpfully.

The three of us began walking along the tarmacked path through the trees. My new companions were both from South America - she from Mexico and he from Colombia, and we chatted about where we had travelled in Spain, my travel experiences in Colombia and any other topics of mutual interest I could come to think of. It wasn't in Spanish, but it was refreshing to have a conversation with individuals who viewed me as an interesting stranger, as opposed to a customer. I realised I had missed it.

The path flattened a little as it began to zigzag up the hill. Judging by the number of people we walked past, we were on the right track and we emerged from the woods by the entrance kiosks of the Alhambra. I was conscious I didn't want to impinge upon my new-found friends' time at Granada's most famous landmark and, although they were touchingly and curiously eager for me to join them on an audio tour of the site, I made my excuses and left them to it. As interesting as it might have been, I didn't fancy traipsing around from audio point one to 25 in a loop with a growing crowd of tourists.

Instead, I walked towards the intimidating stone towers of the citadel. I'd like to claim that I deliberately set out to explore the site in chronological order, but in truth I just went towards the most eye-catching building I could see. Once I'd passed through the tower entrance, I came upon a maze of ruins that showed the foundations of the buildings that had once existed. Around 100 metres away the Watch Tower stood on the western tip of the hill. On a clear day such as this, it was possible from the top of the tower to see the city sprawl for miles into the distance.

Originally constructed as a small castle in the 9th century, the Alhambra was later transformed into a palace and fortress complex. The last of the site's Islamic palaces was built during the decline of the Nasrid dynasty, and as the Spanish monarchy closed in, the area served as a place of refuge for Muslims. Following the city's surrender, the Alhambra became a Royal Court and underwent further changes. The complex bears the fingerprints of so many rulers that, as a visitor, it's difficult to envisage what it looked like at any one time. The nearest building to the citadel was the enormous Renaissance Palace of Charles V. Work on it began in the 16th century and continued intermittently until as recently as 1957. The square palace is built around a vast circular open-air courtyard which today serves as a glamorous event space.

As is so often the case, it is the gardens at the site that will linger longest in my memory. I was serenaded by birdsong as I strolled between the shin-high green hedgerows at the perimeter of each of the heavily manicured flower beds. Somehow, in the adjacent Generalife, the gardens were even prettier. The unusually mundane name, to English eyes at least, of Generalife originates from the Arabic *Jannat al-'Arīf*. This translates as the 'Architect's Garden'. He was one lucky architect.

The space was initially used as the summer palace and country estate of Granada's Muslim rulers, but was allowed to fall into disrepair when the Spanish monarchy took control. The Alhambra suffered a similar fate during the 18th, and early part of the 19th, century. Its previously grand buildings were occupied by thieves and beggars and used to store dung. Remarkably, that wasn't the worst of it. At the end of their short time in control of the city between 1808 and 1812, Napoleon's retreating troops blew up two of the towers.

A smaller, but perhaps more shocking crime was committed by celebrated British travel writer Richard Ford in the 19th century. Following a visit to the landmark, he returned to England with a two-metre long piece of medieval frieze stolen from the Alhambra. Ford then had the cheek to complain in his guidebook about the dilapidated state of the palace. The disappearance of the frieze remained a mystery in Granada until the artefact was recently returned to the Alhambra by Ford's descendants after a 187-year absence.

Although evidence of Moorish influences remain, the authenticity and legitimacy of the renovations of the Generalife over the last two centuries have been questioned. In the mid-19th century the French writer Théophile Gautier complained that 'The delicate sculptures and the marvellous guilloches of this fairy-like architecture have been obliterated, filled up, and engulfed'.

One of the areas that has undergone the most change is the still feted Court of the Water Channel. Colourful flower beds flank the channel, which is less than a metre wide and the length of a swimming pool. It feeds the fountains running down the middle of the quad that create a restful sequence of small arching jets of water. Inevitably, the little courtyard was packed with tourists staring passive aggressively at the back of each others' heads as they competed for space to take the perfect photograph. Which rather seemed to miss the point. To escape the worst of the crowds, I wandered towards the far corners of the gardens and back towards the Alhambra.

By the time I had meandered back, the heat of the day had arrived - and so had the coach tours. I took a final look around and set off downhill, back towards the city centre. To the birds flying high above in the clear blue sky, I must have appeared like a solitary ant, slowly making my way in the opposite direction to the oncoming masses.

After grabbing some lunch and an obligatory ice cream, I returned to my accommodation to collect my things and find a hostel to spend the night. Casting aside memories of the bizarre anomalous experience of my night in the uninhabited hostel in Alicante, I found myself looking forward to the change of pace that living in a shared space with other travellers would bring. I just hoped this change wouldn't involve being awoken innumerable times throughout the night as people came back from their evening escapades.

Years of experience of staying in hostels have taught me six key rules about how best to select a bed:

1. **Choose a mixed dormitory.** Men are smellier, noisier and more obnoxious without the fairer sex around. Female travellers are, by and large, more interesting. There, I said it. The secret's out.

2. **Get there early enough to grab a locker.** Many hostels still don't provide a locker for each guest, and some don't provide any at all.

3. **Choose the top bunk.** A hotly-debated topic, but

to my mind there's no argument. The benefits you get from being able to sit down by your locker are outweighed by the likelihood you will spend the night sleeping underneath a creaking bed that sounds like it could collapse at any moment. It also prevents your bunkmate using your prone body as an additional rung as they climb into bed.

4. **Choose a bed away from the windows.** Firstly, because you're less likely to be disturbed by the street noise. Secondly, because hostel owners are notoriously tight-fisted when it comes to furnishing the rooms. As a result, the curtains are rarely fit for purpose. You'll often find two transparent sheets, barely thicker than tracing paper, hanging loosely from a pole near the ceiling. So if you're by the window, you'll be awake at 5.30am regardless of what time you were kept awake to by your roommates.

5. **Choose a bed away from the entrance to the room.** You want to keep footfall around your bed as minimal as possible. For the same reasons, and more, if there's a bathroom in your room, keep clear of that too.

6. **If you can find a bed that is all of these things, you're in too big a room.** While it's tempting to save a euro by reserving a room containing 10 beds or more, if you're in a popular hostel, you will significantly diminish your chances of getting

a decent night sleep. A four-bed room is intimate, six is ok, eight's the limit.

At the hostel I was given a collection of white sheets to make my bed. My room was empty when I entered, but many of the beds already had items strewn across them. Out of the two that were available, I opted for the bed that had the fewest stains and was situated diametrically opposite the door. To show the bed was now taken, I scattered some of my clothes over it and dumped the rest of my belongings and bed sheets in a locker before heading straight back out to explore more of the streets of Albaicín.

I was admiring the potted geraniums hanging from the balconies, and appreciating the peace away from the crowds at the Alhambra, when I finally came across the viewpoint I had failed to discover the day before.

My only misfortune was arriving 19 years too late. During his time as US president, Bill Clinton watched the sun set from this spot and told journalists afterwards that it was 'the most beautiful sunset in the world'. Unsurprisingly, Granada's tourist board jumped on this quote. When I visited, crowds of tourists jostled for space with traders seeking to sell the castanets, sunglasses and artwork they had laid out on sheets. In the corner of the square, a man sang something indecipherable in a croaky voice as he played his guitar. Any hopes I had harboured of savouring some moments of quiet reflection while absorbing the view quickly evaporated.

I walked back towards the city centre via the Basilica San Juan de Dios. The basilica was built in honour of Joao Duarte Cidade, later known as Juan de Dios or John of God. Joao was a homeless orphan in the early 16th century who became, in turn, a soldier, a bookseller and a health worker. It is in recognition of his last profession that he was named the patron saint of hospitals and the sick.

While I enjoy admiring the beauty and scale of religious landmarks, my curiosity rarely extends to paying to go in. When forced to make a decision between entering and having to eat a banana sandwich for dinner, or alternatively being able to afford a burger, I will, to my shame, usually opt for the latter. My hunger for knowledge has its limits. On this occasion I was convinced to pay the €4 entrance fee by the fact that an audio guide was included. If nothing else, I reasoned, this represented an opportunity to test my Spanish. And if I didn't understand everything, then I'd probably only miss a description about how a painting reflects a Baroque artist's Freudian sentiments towards his mother.

The external appearance of the basilica was unremarkable and my expectations of what was inside had been lowered further by the gambling arcade located opposite it. But inside the church resembled Aladdin's cave. The walls, particularly the extraordinary altarpiece, were practically dripping with gold. I'd never seen anything remotely like it. Every time I tried to listen to the audio guide, I became distracted by another piece of the opulent display. Its intricacies left me feeling sympathy for the cleaners tasked with keeping it so shiny.

The Basilica San Juan de Dios provides a daily soup kitchen to help those in need and there is a hospital built within the grounds. As he grew in prominence, Joao Duarte Cidade organized his followers into the Order of

Hospitallers and after his death the Order was entrusted with the medical care of the Pope. Today, the Order runs more than 300 hospitals located in 53 countries across the world. Yet in spite of all of this altruism, long-held misgivings about ornate religious buildings stirred within me. I couldn't help but look at the ostentatious display of wealth without concluding that toning it down a little could help the Church do even more. A little less inspiration, a little more action. No doubt art historians would beg to differ.

By now it was early evening and I returned to the hostel, where my dormitory was once again empty. I began making a token effort to use the sheets I had been given to make my bed. Halfway through, I was joined in the room by an Argentinian who jumped up to sit on his bed on the top bunk opposite me. It seemed strange to sit in silence, so we made small talk in Spanish about the city, the Alhambra and the large number of tourists milling around. Mainly, I was preoccupied by my ongoing struggle to tuck in the corners of the bed sheet though. As conversation turned to where we both came from, I had a moment of clarity, and suddenly realised how much my Spanish had improved. I was midway through a conversation I both understood and was fully contributing to, while simultaneously carrying out another task altogether.

Trying to learn a foreign language can be a frustrating experience that sometimes feels like a series of missed opportunities. When using Spanish, my thought process often became blocked as I rushed to recall hours of grammar rules while at the same time taking into account the responses of the person I was interacting with. As a consequence, I regularly fell over my words and found it difficult to eloquently express my emotions. But here I was, in the midst of a rare moment of success. I was demonstrating a level of aptitude that even a few weeks ago felt light years away. The conversation continued and I tried hard not to fall from the pedestal I had temporarily placed myself on.

I never found out the Argentinian's name. Names seem so trivial when travelling. It's almost certain your paths won't cross again - particularly when one of you is riding a bicycle - and it's much easier not to worry that you can't remember someone's name if you never exchanged names in the first place. Nevertheless, the joy our conversation brought me will remain with me for years to come.

In contrast, I'm quite sure the Argentinian never thought about our discussion ever again.

19

Granada to Torrox-Costa

Waking early, and knowing instinctively that the reverberating snores of my roommates gave me no chance of falling back to sleep, I packed my bags and got back on the saddle. The plan, as ever, was to get some decent mileage behind me before the sun became too hot, and then cruise downhill all the way to the sea. The Sierra Nevada was a safe distance away to the east and the painful climbs it necessitated were in the past. However, while the Sierra Nevada's reputation precedes itself, it was the far less well-known - make that almost unheard of - Sierras de Tejeda, Almijara y Alhama Natural Park that very nearly proved to be my undoing.

But that was all to come. After leaving the suburbs behind, I was soon travelling through dusty, empty fields.

Every so often I would pass small villages such as cute La Malahá, where the population is counted in hundreds rather than thousands. The size of Agrón, another nearby rural village, is belied by the fact it moved its festival marking the Immaculate Conception of the Virgin Mary (celebrated globally on 8 December) to mid-August in order to ensure enough people are around to attend. Perhaps Christmas comes early there too.

The Duke of Wellington owns a large estate in Agrón, which is remarkable for a number of reasons. Not least because the village doesn't appear big enough for anything large. I hadn't seen a soul in any of the villages I had travelled through, and had put this down to their modest size. The actual reason struck me as I cycled towards Fornes. It was a Sunday.

Losing track of days is one of the welcome side effects of travel. Away from home, it ceases to matter whether it's a Tuesday or a Thursday. I should have learned by now that in the Mediterranean it does matter however if it's a Sunday and you need to go shopping.

Usually, I remembered in time to purchase enough emergency rations on a Saturday to last until I arrived somewhere for dinner the following evening. On this occasion it had entirely slipped my mind and I had only some nuts, an apple and an orange in reserve. With each revolution of the pedals, I was cycling away from shops and deeper into the countryside. Fornes represented my last opportunity to find sustenance until I reached the coast. Once I left the village, I would enter the Sierras de Tejeda, Almijara y Alhama Natural Park, where I'd have as much chance of finding a Bengal tiger as I would a Mercadona.

For once I had made good progress that morning and had covered more than 40km by 11.15am. This created a dilemma. Even if I could find a shop or restaurant in Fornes, it was too early to expect it to be serving customers. I didn't fancy kicking my heels for an hour while I waited to find out if somewhere would open, but on the other hand, I was desperate to avoid crossing the mountains during the hottest part of the day on an empty stomach.

As I turned right off the main road to get to Fornes, I could see that the village was more developed than the others I had passed that morning. It was, unquestionably though, still a village. Located at the bottom of a small hill, its white buildings shone in the sun like a beacon of hope. I approached slowly, scanning side streets for signs of life and found my salvation thanks to the incongruous sight of five very drunk men drinking beer on a small raised patio attached to a bar.

Inside the curtains were drawn, and it took a second or two for my eyes to adjust to the darkness. When my vision returned, I saw a bar in front of me and a broken slot machine sitting idly in the corner. No one was around, but an overpowering smell of cigarette smoke clung to the walls and the faded, flowery upholstery.

'*¿Hola?*' I enquired hopefully.

No one appeared. I began to try again.

'*¿Hol...*'

All of a sudden, a young, plump blonde woman pushed open the door to the kitchen and stood behind the bar.

'*Hola,*' she replied, surprised to see me.

'*¿Puedo ver la carta?* Could I see the menu?

'*Sí, pero no servimos comidas calientes hasta esta tarde. El cocinero llega al mediodía.*' Yes, but we're not serving hot meals until this afternoon. The chef will arrive at noon.

I digested this setback. '*¿Hace sándwiches?*' Do you do sandwiches?

It was the barmaid's turn to pause. I tried to look as kind and earnest as I could as she mulled over the possibility. Finally, she spoke. '*¿Jamón y queso, de acuerdo?*'

'*¡Perfecto! Muchas, muchas gracias.*' I walked back outside, without even enquiring how much the cheese and ham sandwich would cost. Already sorely needed, this purchase transpired to be nothing short of priceless due to the events that unfolded later in the day.

While I waited for the food to be served, I watched the drunken antics of the five men. Normally, watching drunk strangers while sober is irksome and tedious. You have no context for whether they are normal, interesting and intelligent individuals every other day of the year, and take it as read they are always as useless, stupid and obnoxious as they appear at that moment.

Still, I couldn't help but be amused by the befuddled state of the drunkest man. It appeared he was unable to retain more than one thought in his head at any one time. His overriding desire was to smoke a cigarette, yet accomplishing this was beyond him.

I watched him inhale through his mouth as if a cigarette was on his lips. When it slowly dawned on him that he couldn't taste nicotine, he stopped and his head lolled heavily as he looked around with glazed eyes to find where he had put his cigarettes. Upon seeing the packet on the floor by his feet, he bent down to pick them up. As he did so, he fell off his chair and collapsed into a heap on the ground. He lay there for some time before hauling himself back onto his seat, the cigarettes still on the ground. Having completely forgotten about the preceding 30 seconds, he then started sucking through pursed lips again. And so the cycle continued.

Such was their level of intoxication, it took a while before any of his friends even noticed this behaviour. When one did, he walked over, put a cigarette in his friend's mouth and lit it for him. It was a tender moment. Unfortunately, a new thought had evidently entered into the head of the drunkest man, for the cigarette dropped from his lips absentmindedly. His companion chuckled, picked it off the ground and put it back in his friend's mouth like a dummy. The man smiled and tried to speak to thank him, but predictably lost the cigarette in doing so. Deciding that providing further help would be pointless, the swaying assistant gave up. Left alone again, the man then started jabbering animatedly to no one in particular. Intrigued by his passion, I tried to follow his Spanish, but eventually I too gave up. I couldn't understand it and neither, judging by his friends' faces, could they.

After my entertaining lunch, I resumed riding until the tarmac road ran out unexpectedly. In its place was a dusty grey gravel, which I suspected would have the effect of kryptonite on my road bike tyres. Be that as it may, my options were limited. I could either grin and bear the rough ground for the remaining 36km of my intended route through the middle of the Sierras de Tejeda, Almijara y Alhama Natural Park, or I could cycle a circuitous 80km around the circumference of the park, which would take the day's cycle to considerably more than 120km. I wasn't keen on the latter idea and, making peace with the fact that I may have to change my first inner tube of the trip, I opted to stick to the original plan.

It wasn't just a combination of stubbornness and laziness that kept me from altering my route. Many of my favourite moments of the trip had come from taking the road less travelled. It was always slower, but it was safer than cycling on main roads and a hundred times more interesting. Part of my motivation to come to Spain was to spend time in spectacular national parks. The path in front of me may have been laid with hazards rather than gold, but how bad could it be?

I was relieved that my tyres were still intact after 40 minutes of climbing. Progress was slow, but the scenery was beautiful. Pine forest covers the majority of the park's 100,000 acres and I appeared to have it all to myself as I made my way across the limestone hillside. As the trees became sparser and the severity of the ascent increased, it became faster to walk than to cycle. I reminded myself that every step was one closer to the beach. Or at least it would have been had I not missed a turning. Retracing my steps, I found an unmarked trail almost a kilometre back and began pushing my bike towards a viewpoint. There, facing the sea, I surveyed the surrounding mountains. Hundreds of metres downhill, I could see small paths occasionally emerge between the trees. The challenge was working out how to get there.

The problem was compounded by the paucity of defined tracks and an intermittent mobile signal that confused my phone's GPS. My battery was already running low, and I silently congratulated myself for purchasing a power bank in Alicante. Without it, I'd still be on the hillside today. I had shown less foresight with regards to water rationing. I hadn't anticipated being in the mountains so long and my water supply was already dwindling. Resolving to return to civilization as soon as possible, I headed down towards the sea along the widest path I could find.

The terrain became more extreme on the southern face of the mountains. Andalucia's tourist board says the landscape contains 'deep ravines, steep slopes, sharp ridges and rugged crags'. I can vouch for the accuracy of this description. Its almost complete inaccessibility meant that for centuries the area was a haven for bandits and served as a retreat for anti-Nationalist guerrillas during the Civil War. If this doesn't sound like a place ideally suited for a road bike, you'd be right. When configuring the route, the app on my phone had seemingly decided that as the journey could be achieved on foot, it could also be accomplished by bike. I walked down the trail for more than an hour in the baking heat, dragging my sorry bike all the way. The benign grey dust of the ascent had by now been replaced by scree. The slope made it difficult to balance the weight of my panniers and every now and again my rear wheel slipped off the path, causing stones to dislodge and fall around me.

The path was getting wider and deeper so that soon it was roughly a metre wide and a metre deep. I still hadn't seen anyone else in the park, but I took the path's broadening furrow to indicate that it received more footfall than my experience suggested. I came across some fallen trees obstructing the track, but I thought little of them as I carried my bike over them. I hadn't passed any obvious alternative routes, so I resolutely continued my descent. The first alarm bells began to ring when I approached an 8ft drop. Having convinced myself I was on a well-trodden path, this seemed odd, but I reasoned that maybe only hardy hikers came walking here. An 8ft drop might be a major headache for a cyclist, but for hikers it's hardly insurmountable.

Pushing aside any reservations, I lowered my bike down as I leaned over the rock face. The front tyre hung in the air. I couldn't stretch any further, so I dropped the bike as gently as I could onto the ledge below. The rear wheel landed heavily, causing the bike to bounce and jerk in the dust. I dropped down onto the ledge, desperately hoping I hadn't just placed myself into a self-imposed prison. I'd clambered over 8ft walls on obstacle courses before - admittedly more than a decade ago - so I was hopeful I could haul myself back up if necessary. I chose not to dwell on the fact that retrieving the bike would be another matter entirely.

Composing myself, I regathered my stuff and carried on making my way downhill. I had barely been going for five minutes when I saw a gorse thicket in front of me. I realised with a sickening sensation of dread that this wasn't a path at all. I should have suspected it before; the fallen logs were a giveaway. The reason this 'path' looked bigger than any other was that it was, of course, a dried-up riverbed. I walked back up to the rock face I had just descended to assess my options. Poor judgement had left me marooned on a mountain with little water and very little food. I looked at the birds overhead and darkly wondered how long before they would start to circle ominously.

It is in situations like these that people call the mountain rescue service. I promised myself that the circumstances were going to need to get much graver before I did that. If I had to wait until the next day to attract someone's attention, then so be it - it was the least I deserved. I couldn't bear the thought of my name being in the news as the stupid English tourist who got stuck coming down a mountain on a road bike. Besides, I didn't know what number I could call. My power bank had been cheap so I knew it wouldn't last me indefinitely, but it at least bought me some time.

It was clear that the first thing to do was to remove the heavy bags from the pannier rack on the bike. This effectively meant there were three things that I needed to move to the ledge above my head: the pannier bags, the bike and myself. It was like the old riddle where you have to get the fox, the chicken and the sack of grain across the river intact. If I hauled myself out, there was no way I would be able to reach back down to collect the bike and the pannier bags. Conversely, if I chucked the bags over first, but couldn't get myself over the top, I would lose access to all of my remaining food, water and clothes.

The pannier bags weighed a little less than the bike and were certainly a lot easier to throw. This left my bike as the biggest problem. I knew it would be a hollow victory if I escaped without it. Even when I lifted the frame over my head like an Olympic weightlifter, I couldn't get the bike wheels over the lip of the rock shelf. I tried throwing it from this position, but it made little difference. The wheels bounced ineffectually off the rock and the bike fell back, cutting my shins. Short of a serious growth spurt or months in the gym, this technique was doomed to fail.

Trying a different tack, I pushed the bike as high as I could on the dusty slope to my right-hand side. I knew it wouldn't get all the way to the ledge using this method, but if it gave me an angle from which I could at least reach the bike when, if, I myself got to the top, I then would have a chance of retrieving it. But every time I tried, the bike slid back down to my feet, like grains of sand in a hole at the beach. It was exasperating. I tried the other side of the slope where gorse was growing. I had been disinclined to try this side as I was keen to avoid puncturing my tyres, but by this point I knew it was more important to have a bike with a puncture than no bike at all. I placed the front tyre and handlebars on the slope and then pushed the frame up as high as I could from the rear tyre. The bike moved only a little as a branch became snagged between the spokes of the front wheel, but as a consequence, this time the frame stayed in position.

I then picked up my interconnected pannier bags and, using my best hammer throw technique, launched them over the top of the ridge. I must have looked like Miss Trunchball in *Matilda* when she launched that girl out of the window by her pigtails. My bags landed out of sight on the rock above me. This left just me stranded down below. I had planned to use my upper body strength to get my head over the ridge and then do an undignified shuffle to get my legs over. But this turned out to be impossible. Unlike on obstacle courses, this rock face wasn't at a straightforward 90° angle. You might assume this would make it easier to scale, but the fact that the rock was closer to me at the bottom than the top meant I couldn't jump to get the purchase over the edge of the rock that I needed to drag the rest of my body over.

I tried a couple of alternative approaches, scuffing my hands to little avail. My ego had convinced me this would be the easy part. I couldn't work out whether I wished I'd had a friend with me to share in my plight, or whether I was glad to be on my own to save myself the embarrassment. Adopting a new method, I reached for a root growing up the side of the slope. Using this as leverage, I grabbed a branch to the right of the hole and managed to drag myself to the top. The shame of needing to make an emergency rescue call appeared to have subsided. Temporarily overlooking the predicament I still found myself in, I allowed a brief wave of relief to pass over me.

Kneeling on the rocky ledge, I could see my pannier bags covered in dust. Many of my possessions, including an apple, had scattered across the dirt upon impact. Turning around to my bike, I stretched down and grabbed the handlebars. The bike twisted awkwardly as I pulled it up towards me.

It was now past 4pm. I had told my Airbnb host Lucia I would be arriving within an hour, so I sent her a message, as bland as I could manage in the circumstances, to explain that I would be late. I then turned my attention to locating the path I should have taken. Around 100 metres up the mountain, I spotted a single wooden post to my left. It was completely unmarked, and if I hadn't been looking so carefully for something,

160

anything, to guide me, I would have missed it a second time.

I crossed the hillside next to gnarled trees contorted by years of wind exposure. The path, which appeared not to have been used for months, was obscured by dense, spiky gorse which scratched at my arms and legs. Fighting a way through would have been tricky enough if I was hiking, but the need to drag my bike behind me made my limbs look as if they had been attacked by stray cats.

After half an hour, things started to look up when I could see a clearing ahead of me. Approaching it, I could hear the quiet burble of a stream so I turned to reach for a bottle from my bag. As I did so, I realised that one of my pannier bags was open and that one of the plastic bags inside it, which had been hastily packed following my hammer throw over the ridge, was no longer there. It must have got caught on a branch as I made my way through the bushes. A quick inventory revealed I was missing a water bottle, a few bike accessories and the food I had been assiduously rationing. I no longer had the energy for anger, but the loss of these items was undeniably a kick in the teeth. Dusk wasn't far away and the bag could have been anywhere. Going back for it wasn't an option.

I sent another message to Lucia, apologising again that I was late and warning her that, based on my current progress, I wouldn't be arriving any time soon. My early lunch at the bar now seemed a long time ago. Given my difficulties charting a route to the coast, I knew it was essential to get out of the national park before darkness fell. During the hours that followed, I walked in the descending gloom as quickly as the loose ground and my tired legs would allow.

At around 10pm, in the last fragments of light I could just make out a couple of farmhouses in the middle distance. Against the odds, I thought I had made it out of the park in the nick of time. But far from being my salvation, this milestone merely marked a new chapter in this nightmarish saga. At long last, I'd arrived on the sweet even surface of a tarmacked road. It was just a shame the absence of street lights left me virtually blind.

As I was travelling on a shoestring and without the intention of cycling at night, my bike lights were the cheapest money could buy. They were designed to be seen - not to see. In the pitch black I couldn't make out anything more than two metres in front of me. To borrow a Jack Kerouac quote, I was lost in 'the manuscript of a night I couldn't read'. A few houses were dotted around the hillside but these were all built away from the road and their light never reached me. Sensing my presence, dogs barked ferociously nearby and I reacted like a cat on a hot tin roof. I'm an avowed dog lover, but when I was 12 years old I was bitten on the ankle by a small stray dog as I cycled up a hill towards my house. My dad had been with me, but he kept on cycling, leaving me to face the pack of dogs alone. I reminded him of this story the other day.

'I don't remember that at all. I don't believe that happened,' he said dismissively. 'And if it had, you'd have got a tetanus jab.'

'That's exactly what I did get,' I answered indignantly.

'I took him to the doctors for it,' my mum chimed in.

'Oh.' My dad was silent for a few seconds. 'Well, you should have cycled faster then!'

You could argue this story provides an insight into why I was petrified of the dogs above Torrox-Costa. Or you might just come to the conclusion that when you're alone in the dark in the middle of nowhere and you suddenly hear barbarous-sounding dogs of unknown size barking angrily at you from a few metres away, it's terrifying. All I could do was hope each front garden had a gate.

If the local dogs weren't enough to keep me on edge, the road's hairpin bends certainly were. I was worried that having worked so hard to get out of the national park, I would miss a bend in the road and cycle straight over a precipice. From the apex of the bends I could sometimes see the shining lights of the town below. They were gradually getting closer, but as I knew from my experience in the park, seeing something and finding a way to get there were two very different things.

In the hour and a half I spent in the darkness, I saw no more than 10 cars. Each set of glowing headlights provided a precious opportunity to see the layout of the road. However, the appearance of the vehicles was also a reminder of how easily an inattentive driver might veer onto the wrong side of the road. Halfway down the hill, one of the passing cars slowed to a halt next to me. My imagination, which was already running wild with fears of rabid dogs, went into overdrive. If I was kidnapped here, it could be weeks before anyone found me. I certainly wasn't counting on the men I had lunch with to remember me. As my eyes adjusted to the bright headlights, I heard the man turn off his radio and wind down his window.

'*¿Está bien?*' he asked doubtfully. Are you ok?

The innocence of the question caught me off guard. I could feel myself beginning to unravel, the stress of the past few hours bursting to be released. I wanted to tell him I was far from ok, that I'd been trapped up a mountain, I had run out of food and still barely knew where I was. But what help would that do?

So in true English fashion I simply replied, '*Si, gracias,*' as if being out there in the pitch black at 10.45pm was exactly where I wanted to be.

Unsure what to make of me, he shrugged, turned back to look at the road ahead and began to pull away in his car. I was alone again.

By this point I'd drained almost the entirety of both my power bank and my phone battery. I was desperately trying to preserve the last few precious minutes of usage I had left until I really needed them in order to find my accommodation. As I got closer to the coast, the proliferation of roads meant I could no longer simply follow the one I was on. I was forced to pause at every junction, peering through the inky blackness to guess which way was best. But each time I thought I was making progress, I'd end up in a dead end. Confused, I'd shine the torch on my phone over the area like a detective at a crime scene to discover that I had cycled into a cemetery or up someone's drive.

Finally, I saw road signs pointing towards Torrox-Costa for the first time. More significantly, I also reached roads with street lights. Energised by the achievement, I was belatedly able to make some real progress. I was acutely aware that at this late hour there was a chance Lucia might tell me to sling my hook. She patently could have done without the amount of inconvenience I was causing her.

Nearly 45 minutes later I arrived at the small housing estate where Lucia lived. She had big brown eyes and was only a few years older than myself. I was braced for her to give me a fully deserved barrage of criticism, yet she just seemed relieved to see me. I must have looked a mess: weary, enveloped in a layer of dirt and covered in little cuts. I began to apologise profusely, but she gently pointed to her lips and told me the baby was asleep. Tiptoeing round to the side entrance of the property, Lucia explained which keys were for which locks - information which admittedly went straight over my head. The side door took us directly into the annexed pool house and then into the basement where my bed and bathroom were located. She bid me goodnight and I crept into bed. I instantly fell asleep. It was 12.20am.

20

Torrox-Costa

I'm a firm believer in the aphorism *carpe diem*. You can do a lot in a day, and experience a lot during a day of travel. But this was not a day for action.

Predictably, I slept like a log. The house was quiet and the windowless basement ensured my room remained as dark as the roads the night before. It was only the urgent pangs of hunger that eventually roused me. When I entered the empty pool room and saw the sunlight streaming in through the large conservatory windows, it felt like I had woken up in an entirely different world.

As I walked down to the Mercadona in the town centre just after midday, I calculated that I'd consumed only 200 calories in the previous 24 hours. I had no idea how many I'd expended, but it was time to make up some of the deficit. Sitting on the wide, sandy beach I set about carb loading with relish. Like a python that hasn't eaten for months and then swallows a deer, I didn't move much after that.

Torrox-Costa is a perfectly pleasant, if unremarkable, place. The town is little known outside the region and has a much lower profile than its coastal neighbours which include Malaga, Torremolinos and Almería. As a result, there was international bemusement when researchers announced that in a study of European beach resorts, little Torrox-Costa was found to have the best climate. So next time people smugly tell you they're heading off to Marbella, you can tell them to stick that in their pipe and smoke it.

Torrox-Costa came out on top thanks to its warm, dry and moderate climate. Temperatures don't rise higher than 32°C, nor fall below 10°C. And while it rains only 54 days a year, the town never experiences droughts due to the precipitation that falls over the Sierras de Tejeda, Almijara y Alhama Natural Park.

I sat on the beach enjoying the sun while I called home and studied Spanish. The celebrated weather clouded over in the late afternoon, so I walked to the 19th century lighthouse at the far end of the esplanade before eating dinner under the plastic marquee of a seaside restaurant. The wind, which a few hours before had been non-existent, was now whipping off the sea and whistled as it rattled the restaurant's flimsy structure. I returned to my accommodation for an early night, happy to have the option to do so.

21

Torrox-Costa to Malaga

After the debacle of two days before, I needed to regain my cycling mojo. On paper, the journey to Malaga seemed perfect: a straightforward 50km ride that, for the most part, ran parallel to the coastline. I imagined myself cruising triumphantly into the city, where my mum was flying out to meet me the following day.

In practice, although the road between Torrox-Costa and Malaga was usually only metres away from the shore, it wasn't all that pretty. To my disappointment, the beaches were not one infinite strip of sand, but a series of poky outbreaks of shingle, separated by rocky headland and private properties. Perhaps I had been spoiled by the abundance of beaches in recent weeks. Either way, the road was not one to dawdle on. A constant flow of vehicles sped past, while powerful crosswinds lingered from the night before, hampering my progress.

The app on my phone suggested I could avoid the main road by taking a horseshoe-shaped detour about a third of the way along the journey. I was wary of trusting the app again, but by the time I reached the proposed turning I was eager to travel inland to escape the traffic.

As I cycled up a hill directly into the morning sunlight, I saw two black objects at the summit. I was reminded of an occasion a few months earlier in Panama. I had been cycling downhill on a hopelessly rusty fixed gear bike I'd rented from a street corner, when I saw a strange, stationary brown object in the middle of the road. The single-track road cut straight through the rainforest, so I assumed the object was a big, crinkly leaf that had fallen from the canopy. Like a toddler stamping in puddles, I quite fancied hearing the satisfying crunch of a dry leaf under my tyre and steered towards it.

Generally, fixies don't have brakes - the only way to stop is to apply backwards pressure on the pedals which, as anyone who has ever tried it knows, is easier said than done when you're going at speed. For no specific reason, at the last second I had a moment of uncertainty and aborted my trajectory to evade the object. As I did so, it moved, almost imperceptibly. I stopped abruptly, realising upon closer inspection it was a sloth. Relief coursed through me. If I had run over this docile creature while seeking the fleeting pleasure of a vegetative crunch, I wouldn't have been able to look myself in the mirror. To ensure it avoided any other potential accidents, I remained with the sloth until it had finished crossing the road and was safely halfway up a nearby tree. Suffice to say, I was there for some time.

Recalling this experience, I hoped something similarly heartwarming would be waiting at the top of the hill. Could it be a couple of sunbathing black piglets? Most likely, it would be nothing more than two piles of horse manure. Still, my curiosity was piqued and I raced to the top. When I got there, I recoiled in horror. The objects I had seen were the bodies of two kittens that had been flattened by a car. When I was 10 years old, my family rescued a cute black kitten. My mum, sister and I all loved him, but my dad was less convinced so we named the new addition Marmite. I couldn't help but imagine him here, blissfully unaware of the danger as he played in the sun with a sibling.

They were far from the only roadkill I saw on the trip. In fact, the amount of roadkill I passed was one of the things that most surprised me. I guess you don't think about how many dead animals you will come across when you're planning the road trip of a lifetime. Even more than the quantity, it was the variety of the victims that shocked me. The kittens may have affected me the most, but I also passed dead squirrels, rabbits, pigeons, lizards and mice. I passed a couple of dead snakes too. At least I'm fairly certain they were dead. I wasn't going to hang around to find out.

Leaving the flat cats behind, I completed the detour and returned to the main road. On the outskirts of Rincón de la Victoria I came upon a Mercadona superstore and pulled into the car park to buy lunch. As I did so, I passed a homeless man playing a guitar next to a cardboard sign bearing the words 'I've already got an arsehole'. I didn't stop to chat.

Rincón de la Victoria is said to have the highest income per capita in Andalucia. This is in large part because it is home, or indeed the second home, to the great and the good of Malaga. In summer the number of Spaniards seeking respite from the city heat causes the town's population to treble. I had only intended to stay for a short while, but lying in the sun on the beach, I told myself that my mum wouldn't want me to see too much of Malaga without her. I soon fell asleep.

Back in the land of the living, I began the remaining 15km, which was almost entirely pedestrianised. After cycling along the grand esplanade at Rincón de la Victoria, I was surprised to arrive at the entrance of a dark tunnel cut through the headland. I peered in warily and could only just see the light at the other end. The air temperature was noticeably cooler inside the tunnel, which was barely wide enough for two people to walk side-by-side. Electric lights had been installed, but they were dimly lit and provided limited assistance when navigating around the cold puddles on the stony floor.

Out the other side, I appreciated feeling the warmth of the sun on my back again. But it wasn't long before I was heading back into darkness. The tunnel I had travelled through turned out to be the first in a series of tunnels along this stretch of coastline. They were built at the start of the 20th century to accommodate the train track running between Malaga and Vélez-Málaga, nearly 40km to the east, which was in operation until 1968. Cycling through the tunnels brought to mind four-time Tour de France winner Chris Froome, who in 2014 became the first person to cycle through the Channel Tunnel. Promoting the historic event, he described it as 'an incredible experience'. However, having watched the footage of him passing miles of pipelines and reinforced concrete, it's difficult not to conclude the cycle was actually far less interesting than most people's daily commute.

Emerging from the tunnels, I noticed the shadows were lengthening, but I was reluctant to hasten my pace as I passed a succession of sandy beaches with palm trees, outdoor exercise equipment and seaside cafes. Following the agonising climbs and unmarked tracks of recent weeks, it was a joy to be on such an attractive, flat and navigable route. There were also countless thatched beach shacks, which are commonly referred to as *chiringuitos*. Next to many of these, fires were lit in pits dug into the sand. At the perimeter of each one, skewers of five or six sardines were stuck into the ground. Known as *un espeto*, these skewered sardines are a signature dish for Malagueños. Indeed, one of Malaga's 15 beaches is called *El Dedo* (The Finger) because Alfonso XII, while visiting the city in the 19th century, had to be gently told to ditch the cutlery and eat the sardines with his fingers.

To my disappointment, I later found out that I had passed this waterfront a fraction too early to see the local phenomenon of the *Ola del Melillero*. At around 7.30pm every day, large waves appear without warning, generated far out to sea by the arrival of a high-speed ship into Malaga. The waves routinely swamp the towels and picnic blankets of unsuspecting day-trippers. Watching the shock on the faces of the sunbathers has become a regional pastime and videos showcasing it on YouTube receive millions of views.

As tanned individuals honed their perfect figures on

exercise apparatus and others sat with friends drinking and eating fried fish, it was hard to imagine that life wasn't always thus. But in 1937 the Massacre of the Malaga-Almería highway, regarded as one of the biggest atrocities of the Spanish Civil War, took place along this coastline. When Malaga fell to Franco's Nationalist troops, an estimated 150,000 Republicans fled east towards Almería. En route, they were targeted by aerial and naval bombardments, which killed around 5,000 people, the majority of them civilians.

I cycled into Malaga along the seafront next to the city's ever popular La Malagueta beach. It was no longer warm enough to sunbathe, but that was of little importance to the groups of teenagers cavorting on the sand. I wanted to stop and savour the atmosphere of bonhomie, but there was a more pressing issue at hand. Ever since my time in the Sierras de Tejeda, Almijara y Alhama Natural Park my front wheel had been making an odd noise.

Recalling the failure of my previous calamitous attempts to mend my bike, I resolved to visit a bike shop to get it looked at by someone who knew what they were doing. Unsurprisingly, when examined by an expert, the bike was easily fixed. I tried to ascertain how they had remedied the problem, but, not for the first time, I found that while my Spanish skills were improving, my vocabulary didn't yet extend to the most intricate components of a bicycle.

My Airbnb host for the night, Sandra, was a stout woman in her forties who lived in an unassuming flat with her two cats. The animals couldn't have been more different. One was a cute, inquisitive kitten who jumped in my pannier bags as I unpacked my stuff. The other cat was much older and hissed at me when I tried to say hello. You can guess who spent the night curled up in my room.

22

Malaga

As planned, my mum arrived the next day. Taking one look at my skinny frame, she vowed to get some decent meals in me. Having spent weeks on a diet consisting predominantly of bread, bananas, nuts and oranges, I wasn't going to argue. As such, the next four days took on the form of a holiday rather than a foreign adventure. While relaxing in Malaga, I worried that I'd go soft and baulk at the thought of resuming my journey once my mum had returned home.

I always find it difficult assimilating back into life after travelling by myself. I become so used to doing what I want, when I want, how I want, that virtues such as patience and compromise, both of which I normally possess in shorter supply than I should anyway, take a while to re-emerge. Nonetheless, my mum and I had a wonderful four days walking through the city streets, eating ice creams and looking at the cruise ships in the harbour. I wanted my mum to have the chance to enjoy the beaches I had cycled past en route to the city and it was fun to be one of those people tucking into the freshly caught fried fish, instead of the hungry cyclist watching on from the sidelines.

During our time in Malaga we visited the city's botanical gardens. The park has existed for more than 150 years and now contains in excess of 2,000 plant species. Which is quite an achievement for a site originally used as a recreational farm. So often havens of tranquility in the centre of bustling cities, the botanical gardens in Malaga are located 7km out of town. A fair walk from the nearest bus stop, it's safe to say that no one arrives here by accident. Away from the tourist trail, my mum and I had nearly all 23 hectares of the garden to ourselves. At its southernmost point is the circular pavilion that has come to symbolise the gardens. Built at the far end of a rectangular pool of water, it looks out to the city and the sea below. Decades ago, it would have been a majestic view, but now the tarmacked artery of a motorway blots the panorama.

Back in the city centre, we visited Gibralfaro Castle and the adjacent alcazaba. Built atop of a hill, the walk up to the castle provided excellent views of the baroque city hall and the bullring. We could see the cruise ships in the harbour too, and the observation wheel, which has since been pulled down to make space for a car park. This decision must have caused consternation in the offices of Malaga's tourism board, because when we were there the attraction was one of the centrepieces of the city's marketing content.

The castle was built in the 10th century and is most famous for being the scene of a three-month long siege instigated by the Spanish monarchy against the Muslim population in 1487. The siege turned the castle's exceptional defensive location from an asset into its achilles heel. The inhabitants soon began to starve and ate cats and dogs to survive before they ultimately surrendered. The Siege of Malaga has broader significance as it was not only the first conflict around the world in which both sides used gunpowder, but also the first in which dedicated vehicles were used for the purpose of carrying casualties.

After walking around the crenellated walls of the castle, we strolled around the intricate stone arches and relaxing gardens of the alcazaba below. At the bottom of the hill lies a Roman amphitheatre. Built in the 1st century BC, it is the city's oldest monument. It was found in 1951 when efforts were under way to build a cultural centre on the site. Work was briefly paused to allow archaeologists to begin digging, but construction work resumed and the planned centre was built anyway, the council apparently unaware of the irony of a cultural centre impeding the discovery of the very thing it was set up to promote. Common sense prevailed in 1994, when the centre was demolished to allow a thorough excavation to take place.

Finally, we visited the Picasso Museum, which was one of many in the area dedicated to celebrate Malaga's most famous son. Or to give him his full name, Pablo Diego José Francisco de Paula Juan Nepomuceno María de los

Remedios Cipriano de la Santísima Trinidad Mártir Patricio Clito Ruiz y Picasso. I doubt even his mother used it when he was in trouble.

Visits to famous art museums regularly leave me with mixed emotions. Often, I feel obliged to go, for fear that I will in future be rebuked with a comment such as 'Imagine going to the birthplace of Picasso and not seeing his art!'. In many ways, such criticism is fair - as much as I liked Malaga, it was unlikely I would be back soon, so it was only right to fully explore the city and the stories of the people who have lived there. Yet, despite entering galleries with an open mind, I frequently become disinterested after half an hour and head for the nearest exit, feeling underwhelmed and uncultured.

The Picasso museum would, I hoped, be different. It was located just around the corner from where he was born in the beautifully renovated Buenavista Palace. Arguably, no other painter or sculptor has achieved the level of fame in their own lifetime that Picasso accomplished. As the BBC arts editor Will Gompertz asserts, 'He was a brilliant artist who happened to be in the right place at the right time to respond to the provocation of the camera, aeroplanes, and huge political and social shifts. The way we saw the world changed comprehensively over a few decades, and Picasso reflected that like no other artist.' Picasso's celebrity transcended the art world. His life became the topic of almost as much conversation as his art. He had a string of relationships throughout his life and his infidelity, often with women far younger than himself, intrigued and appalled many.

At one stage, Picasso was even accused of stealing the

Mona Lisa from the Louvre. He was one of several high-profile suspects, including JP Morgan, who were initially thought to be behind the disappearance of the painting in 1911. The mystery surrounding the greatest art theft in history lasted for more than two years until the culprit, a thief named Vincenzo Peruggia, was caught trying to sell the painting to an art dealer in Florence. In the intervening time, the artwork, which was only moderately famous before, had been transformed into the most famous painting in the world. It seems strange to imagine now that the painting is so ubiquitous, but before the theft, 'The *Mona Lisa* wasn't even the most famous painting in its gallery, let alone in the Louvre' according to historian James Zug. Following the heist, more people came to see the empty hooks where the *Mona Lisa* had hung, than had visited the painting when it was on the wall. Indeed, media coverage of the case was so extensive that by the time the painting was found, everyone knew what it looked like.

While not quite as iconic as Mona Lisa's smile, Picasso's most famous works are also known the world over. His painting, *Guernica*, which depicts the German bombing of the Spanish town during the civil war, is evocative of the conflict's brutality. Picasso lived the majority of his life in France and was a staunch opponent of General Franco. When *Guernica* was exhibited in the US to raise money for Spanish refugees of the civil war, Picasso requested that the Museum of Modern Art (MoMA) in New York kept hold of the painting until liberty and democracy had returned to Spain. A few years after the war ended, Picasso joined the French Communist Party and received numerous accolades from party officials, such as the Stalin Peace Prize in 1950 and the Lenin Peace Prize in 1962. However, according to French poet and playwright Jean Cocteau, Picasso became disillusioned by his fellow communists. He is said to have remarked, 'I have joined a family, and like all families, it's full of shit'.

The artist's global fame has contributed to the idea that all of his work is inescapably brilliant. Of course, many of his exhibits are worthy of the acclaim they receive. But Picasso was a phenomenally prolific artist, creating more than 50,000 pieces of art in his lifetime and it stretches credibility to suggest that all 50,000 deserve such praise. To my uninformed eye, a fair few in the museum seemed bang average. These included a display of pictures with unremarkable smudges and lines that, were it not for the fact that they were drawn by Picasso, no one would look at twice. Yet each drawing was accompanied by a lengthy description extolling its virtues.

'I could have done that,' I muttered quietly to my mum.

She laughed, agreeing it wasn't much to look at.

Our heresy must have been overheard. I turned to see a woman in her fifties tutting disdainfully in our direction.

When Picasso was asked to explain the symbolism displayed in his painting *Guernica*, he replied, 'It isn't up to the painter to define the symbols...The public who look at the picture must interpret the symbols as they understand them.' That, in a nutshell, is my problem. I've never been very good at reading the writing on the wall. This isn't to say I didn't find some art that I liked. I could happily have followed Vincenzo Peruggia's lead and walked off with a sculpture called *Bull's Head*. It's a wonderfully simplistic design where the handlebars and saddle of a rusted bike have been welded together so that the saddle resembles the bull's skull and the handlebars represent its horns. Inevitably, there was a weighty explanation of the artwork's meaning next to the sculpture. But I preferred Picasso's summary of how it came to be: 'One day, in a pile of objects all jumbled up together, I found an old bicycle seat right next to a rusty set of handlebars.'

That evening I bid my mum farewell. As she travelled to the airport to fly back home, I headed out in search of food. Now I was paying again, I was operating on a tighter budget than over the past few days. I settled on a restaurant offering two burgers for the price of one and made my order at the till. When the burgers arrived, the waitress was horrified to realise they were both for me. I laughed congenially, but I preferred the reaction my rapacious appetite had received from the students in Granada.

23

Malaga to Fuengirola

After my time relaxing in Malaga, I was fortunate that the next leg of the journey would, I hoped, allow me to ease back into the cycling routine. It promised to be a gentle 33km along the coast to the former tourist hotspot of Fuengirola. As I wasn't travelling far, I started late and by the time I arrived at the long, sandy beaches of western Malaga, the waterfront was already thronging with life. It was a sunny Saturday morning and toned runners wearing only minimal clothing competed for space with young families out on their bikes. The promenade is named in honour of arguably Malaga's second-most famous son, Antonio Banderas. The Oscar-nominated actor, star of classic films such as *The Mask of Zorro*, recently drew widespread acclaim for his portrayal of fellow local boy, Picasso.

While weaving through the crowds I was distracted by the sight of people playing a sport I'd never seen before. It appeared to be a cross between tennis and squash, played by four people in a cage. They were hitting a tennis ball with an object resembling a compressed tennis racquet, which had the depth of a frying pan and in place of strings had small holes like a cheesegrater. If it sounds comical, the fiercely competitive matches were anything but. On my return to the UK, I mentioned this curious spectacle to a friend who works in sports administration. He identified the sport as padel and explained how, as part of his job, he had been assisting efforts to improve the game's international standing. He has his work cut out.

Although there is a padel world championship, in the nearly 30 years that the tournament has been held, the winners of the men's and women's cup have been from either Argentina or Spain. Which isn't quite as bad as the US calling its Major League Baseball championship the World Series, but it hardly screams of global appeal. My friend also explained the rules. The scoring is the same as tennis and you lose the point if the ball bounces twice on the ground, if it strikes you or your partner, or if it directly hits the walls of the opponents' court without first landing on their side of the court. Serves are hit underarm. It looked a lot of fun and would certainly improve a tennis player's ability at the net. If I ever move to Malaga, you'll find me on these courts.

A little further on I came to a 100-metre tall brick chimney in the middle of the esplanade. Built as part of a lead smelting factory in the early 1920s, when Malaga's seafront was dominated by industry, it was redundant 50 years later when demand for lead fell sharply. The factory was subsequently demolished, but the chimney remained, an unloved relic of the city's polluted past. One night in 1993, a broken-hearted romantic named Carlos changed this. Following an argument with his girlfriend, he sought to win her back by abseiling down the chimney with the idea of writing 'Monica, I love you' in white paint. Unfortunately, he ran out of paint, so was only able to write 'Monica'. The next morning, Carlos' act was the talk of the town and the chimney has been known as Monica Tower ever since. His gesture was well received by Monica herself and the couple are now married with two children.

My picturesque route ended abruptly when I was forced inland to cross a bridge over the Guadalhorce River. This doesn't sound too unpleasant, except for the fact that the only nearby bridges were on motorways. Intriguingly, while motorways are no-go areas for cyclists in the UK, the rules are more nuanced in Spain. Here, there are two types of motorways: *autovias* and *autopistas*. Cyclists are permitted to ride on the hard shoulders of *autovias* when there are no alternative routes close by, but are always prohibited from riding on *autopistas*. In practice, the two motorways look much the same, with the *autovia* over the Guadalhorce accommodating four lanes of traffic flowing in either direction.

Cycling on such a road was foolhardy at best. That being said, it was much more direct. Either I set off upstream on a 36km detour to cross a bridge with a dual carriageway, or I cycled along the motorway in front of me for 1km to get to the same place. The extra time on the road probably meant that the longer route was actually more dangerous. So I set off on the motorway and hoped luck was with me. The hard shoulder on the bridge was less than 2ft wide so I hugged the road barrier like a child with a hot water bottle on a winter's night.

The cars nearest to me may have been travelling in the slow lane, but they overtook me at frightening speed. In spite of myself, I hunched my shoulders and tucked my arms into my sides to make myself as small as possible. As I did so, I realised how futile such behaviour was. My pannier bags stuck out far more than my shoulders. I focused instead on doing the only thing I could in the circumstances: getting to the junction on the other side of the bridge as fast as possible. Arriving on the opposing riverbank, I pulled over straight away and carried my bike up the stairs of a footbridge spanning the motorway. I then cycled through some scrubland and a retail park to get to Torremolinos.

When Spaniards think about the English in Torremolinos, they picture heavy-drinking, sunburned holidaymakers. The behaviour of some of these individuals has tarnished the resort's reputation, yet these tourists have simultaneously sustained the local economy. Few Spaniards recall the contribution of the generous Mancunian who played a pivotal role in the town's growth. Severely injured during the Boer War, Sir George Langworthy moved with his Indian-born wife to Torremolinos in the mid-1890s. Sir George was both fabulously wealthy and a devout Christian. Following his wife's premature death at the age of 40, he would give a peseta to anyone who read a Bible passage aloud to him. This habit saw him gain the moniker of *El Ingles de la*

Peseta. Having given away the equivalent of approximately £40 million, by the end of the 1920s he was broke and unable to pay his staff.

To resolve the situation, Sir George handed over the lease of his property to his workers, who planned to turn it into the Costa del Sol's first hotel. Sir George's only condition was that he was supported until his death. They agreed and the hotel soon welcomed high-profile guests such as Salvador Dali and Picasso. Sadly, the hotel is no longer open, but the spark that ignited Torremolinos' tourism industry had been lit.

The town's reputation continued to grow in the decades that followed. In the 1950s Torremolinos was the place to be seen, with celebrities such as Rita Hayworth, Marlon Brando and Grace Kelly coming to stay. It seems remarkable in retrospect, but the arrival of international stars was not always viewed in a positive light by residents. When Brigitte Bardot sunbathed nude, locals wrote a letter of complaint to Malaga's mayor who publicly called for Bardot to be deported due to her 'immoral behaviour and attitude'. How times change. Bardot now has a street in Torremolinos named after her.

Drawn by its glamorous reputation, thousands of tourists capitalised on the falling cost of flights to travel to the resort. Between 1953 and 1959 six hotels opened in Torremolinos. By 1965 the number of hotels had increased more than ninefold. However, when resorts in Greece, Turkey and Morocco grew in popularity during the 1970s and 1980s, Torremolinos was left in their wake. A place, truth be told, where it remains. The town is full of run-down cafes adorned with worn plastic seats. If Benidorm was hilariously naff, then Torremolinos was just naff. As I walked through the streets while trying to ignore the crowds of British tourists and expats, marked out by their red skin, wobbly tattooed stomachs and angry exchanges with relatives, it was hard to imagine that Torremolinos had once been the epitome of cool. In its defence, few people come here to see the town, which is now full of shops from the UK high street such as Costa Coffee, Holland & Barrett and WH Smith. The beach will always be Torremolinos' calling card and its 8km of sand provided ample space to enjoy it.

Fuengirola is located 16km south-west, along a coastal road with gentle undulating hills. The sea's myriad shades of blue shimmered in the sunlight, but what I'll remember most about that short leg of the journey was the game of cat and mouse I had with a chubby, middle-aged man on a very expensive bike. He couldn't bear to behind me and repeatedly went downhill as fast as he could to get back in front. At first, I tried to rise above participating in such a juvenile contest, but having had only my own thoughts for company for miles on end, I couldn't resist picking up the gauntlet. Besides, this race was rigged in my favour. Even with my bags, I was able to conquer the hills much faster than he could. Seeing how this bruised his ego, I stepped it up a notch. I increased the cadence of my pedalling as I came uphill behind him, pausing my pedalling just before I drew level with him so that it appeared effortless as I passed him on the slope. Irked by his own inability to keep up, he would then once again furiously dive down the other side of the hill to get a head start before the next incline. Games such as these are commonplace among cycling commuters as they help journeys to rattle along and before I knew it I was crossing the finish line, victorious, at Fuengirola.

I was worried the town, another resort with its heyday behind it, would display similar signs of decay to those I'd found in Torremolinos. It too had grown exponentially from a small fishing village to a major tourist destination in a short space of time. The town's population had risen from 8,000 in 1960 to more than 30,000 by 1981. Its ambitions had changed accordingly, as demonstrated by Fuengirola's appearance on the 1984 Formula 1 calendar. Budget restraints meant that the race never happened, but it was fun to wander along the seafront, imagining the street circuit that might have been.

Perhaps because Fuengirola never quite reached the dizzying, era-defining heights of Torremolinos, neither has it experienced the lows of its neighbour either. The atmosphere seemed more convivial and the town's British demographic, while certainly present, was far more diluted. I bought an ice cream and walked a couple of miles along the promenade in the late afternoon sun. I passed countless *chiringuitos* on the beach and several sporadic plantations of deckchairs with thatched circular awnings. The vast majority were unused, set up in preparation for the imminent arrival of families during the school holidays. Two thirds of the way along the esplanade was a 25ft high sculpture, commemorating the now defunct currency of the peseta. It was interesting to look at, but felt a little parochial. If the UK had gone the same way as Spain and joined the Euro in 2002, would we now see similar tributes to the pound in places such as Margate? If the Brexit vote is anything to go by, almost certainly.

I walked on a little further and ate dinner at one of

the low-cost beachside restaurants. By Spanish standards, it was still early for dinner and most of the tables were empty. I was served by an attentive young waiter unnecessarily dressed in black tie. It was unclear to me who would come to a beach resort, choose to eat at one of the cheapest restaurants and then feel disappointed by the fact the staff weren't wearing bow ties. As he brought out some bread (free additional bread - what a result!) he told me I was very handsome. I assumed I must have misheard or failed to translate his words correctly, so I pretended not to have heard. When he brought out some seafood tapas from the set menu, he repeated the sentiment for a second time. By the third time he said it, there was no room for doubt. I didn't want to be rude by rejecting his compliments, but I wasn't sure if he thought I was simply playing hard to get. Either way, it left me uncertain how much of a tip to leave.

Flattered, if confused, I walked back along the shore to pick up my bike and head to the Airbnb I had reserved for the next two nights. As was often the case, it was tricky to find and my bike had to be wedged vertically in order for it to fit into the small lift in the apartment block. I was staying in a third floor flat with a stocky man in his thirties called Alejandro. He was friendly, but was visibly impeded by a broken leg sustained in a recent motorbike accident. It made me recall a famous quote from the Australian writer Colin Bowles: 'Why not buy your son a motorbike for his last birthday?' I decided it wasn't the time to share such wisdom.

Alejandro was keen to show me around the next day, but I demurred as watching him painfully try to manoeuvre around furniture suggested he was in greater need of a live-in carer than an adventurous guest.

24

Fuengirola to Marbella

While other resorts live off past glories and nostalgia, Marbella is still in vogue. But quite what the city's affluent crowd would make of my bedraggled, unshaven appearance and sweaty gym shirts remained to be seen.

An *autovia* ran parallel to the shore between Fuengirola and Marbella, so I cut inland to avoid it for as long as possible. Away from the beach, it was amazing how quickly the traffic disappeared. There was a simple reason for this: there was nothing there. Other than miles of dusty grassland, all I saw was a golf course, a forgotten cemetery and a disused dog racing track.

Returning to the coast at La Cala de Mijas, I discovered a boardwalk running over the sand. The indescribable joy of walking in the sun on planks of wood constructed a foot off the ground defies explanation. I assumed the boardwalk would run out within a couple of hundred metres, but to my delight it extended over a far longer distance. It is part of an ambitious, government-sponsored project to create a coastal path that will eventually run for 180km along the length of the Costa del Sol. So in a few years' time you could, in theory, cycle across the region without having to travel on roads at all. Except you won't be able to, as bikes are set to be banned along most of the route. Seeing the empty boardwalk ahead of me, I pretended I hadn't seen the signs prohibiting bikes and savoured the sea breeze on my face as the tyres made a rhythmical, rickety noise across the decking.

When the boardwalk ran out, I hesitantly diverted onto a busy dual carriageway for eight stressful kilometres. I had intended to travel a greater distance on the road, but my nerves were completely shot, so I left the traffic behind and began weaving my way through various housing estates. Progress was slow and involved umpteen wrong turns as I painstakingly negotiated my way around the cul-de-sacs. Preoccupied as I was by looking at both the map and the road in front, I failed to see a large pothole before it was too late.

I heard a sudden ping, followed by the sound of scratching metal. I immediately feared I would have to walk the remaining 9km to Marbella. Looking down, I saw the noise had been caused by a snapped spoke in my rear wheel that had twisted around the spokes next to it. Although the bike was designed to have a pannier rack fitted, the manufacturers probably imagined it would be used to carry lightweight shopping, not 11kg of paraphernalia across wildly varying terrain. So even with the regular check-ups en route, the wear on some of the bike's components was beginning to show.

A broken spoke would not, I hoped, be an insurmountable hurdle. After all, the wheel had another 27 of them. The problem was that now one spoke had broken, it was a ticking time bomb until more followed suit, making the wheel unrideable. I didn't have any metal cutters to remove the snapped spoke, so I bent it around the one next to it and then secured it with tape. Tentatively, I got back on the saddle, and thankfully it seemed to hold.

***

Marbella has carefully cultivated an image of prosperity, but by early 2006 it was practically bankrupt. This is in spite of the fact that famous and wealthy clientele such as Prince Fahd of Saudi Arabia, whose 1,000-strong retinue would routinely spend up to €5 million per day, had been visiting the resort for decades. So where had all the money gone? The answer, as Spanish police have been finding out ever since they launched their wide-ranging investigation, was into brown paper bags. In 1991 a colourful (read racist) mayor called Jesús Gil swept to power in Marbella. Books and TV documentaries have been dedicated to Gil's life, which contain several incidents that would make even Donald Trump blush.

Gil was sent to prison in 1971 after he was found culpable in the deaths of 58 people crushed by shoddy building work carried out by his construction company.

His influential connections led him to receive a pardon from Franco 18 months later. Such a conviction would usually represent an insurmountable stain to the reputation of an individual seeking public office, but Gil resurrected his career to wield far-reaching power as the mayor of Marbella and owner of Atlético Madrid football club during the 1990s and early 2000s. He was sent to prison twice more for crimes of corruption and embezzlement before his death in 2004.

The nefarious system he had built would outlast him, and the city's three subsequent mayors prior to 2006 all spent time in prison on similar charges. The problem was so endemic that the Spanish government was forced to intervene. It ordered the dissolution of the city council, an unprecedented act in the democratic, post-Franco era. The investigation into financial misconduct in Marbella is still under way and has so far seen police seize goods worth €2.4 billion.

But Gil didn't start the fire. Many cities projecting a perception of affluence have unpalatable underbellies and Marbella has attracted more insalubrious characters than most. In the aftermath of World War II, the resort became a haven for prominent Nazis. One such figure was Wolfgang Jugler, Adolf Hitler's chief personal bodyguard. Another was Léon Degrelle, a feted Belgian politician who collaborated and fought alongside the Germans. Degrelle maintained a high profile as a far-right campaigner until his death. His views were largely tolerated, with the notable exception of when he was found guilty of Holocaust denial by the Spanish Supreme Court in 1991 after a survivor of Auschwitz, Violeta Friedman, took legal action against him.

When asked outside the court if he had any regrets about the war, Degrelle responded defiantly, 'Only that we lost!'.

Another Nazi, Otto-Ernst Remer, spent the last few years of his life in Marbella. Remer had arrested the architects of the famous 20 July plot that had failed to assassinate Hitler in 1944. Following the war, he too was a vocal advocate of extreme right-wing policies. He fled to Marbella in the 1990s to avoid a German prison sentence having been found guilty of Holocaust denial and inciting racial hatred.

Learning of his arrival in Spain, Friedman commented, 'This man should be extradited. I feel like I'm living under Franco again, in a country that remains a paradise for Nazi refugees.' If it is unsurprising that former Nazis were protected while Franco was alive, the fact they remained at liberty after his death was because, according to Friedman in 1994, 'the Spanish judicial system remains riddled with old *Franquistas* (Franco supporters)'. That these Nazis were able to enjoy the sunshine lifestyle of the Costa del Sol until their deaths at the ages of 89 (Jugler) and 85 (Degrelle and Remer) certainly sticks in the craw.

Another controversial figure was US billionaire businessman Marc Rich, who in the 1980s bought a house in Marbella. He used it to claim Spanish citizenship and renounced his American citizenship after being indicted on federal charges of tax evasion and of making oil deals with Iran during the country's hostage crisis. If found guilty, he faced more than 300 years in prison. Rich avoided jail in large part thanks to the controversial presidential pardon he was granted on Bill Clinton's last day in office. According to Clinton, the pardon was completely unrelated to the donations made by Rich's wife, which included $450,000 to the Clinton Library and $100,000 to Hillary Clinton's campaign to become a Senator. Others weren't convinced, and an editorial in the New York Times described the pardon as 'a shocking abuse of presidential power'.

Even so, if you're playing Marbella Top Trumps with the criminal underworld, Osama bin Laden is your man. Although he doesn't appear in the holiday brochures, in the 1980s the bin Ladens were regular visitors to 'Marbs', as they almost certainly didn't call it. And to think that I cringed at some of the current clientele.

Maybe because I was expecting a Spanish equivalent of Monaco, to begin with I was underwhelmed by Marbella's charms. It may hold greater cache, but the fact is that Marbella's seafront isn't much different to that of Fuengirola or many other places along the coast. Having said this, the resort grew on me as I explored the old town and its pretty labyrinthine streets around the Plaza de los Naranjos. The 15th century plaza was designed to be Marbella's urban hub and it continues to serve this purpose today. The small square was heaving with tourists amidst the orange trees and orange awnings of the competing restaurants. Not only were the prices exorbitant, and spare seats at a premium, but the sheer density of people meant that while those with seats were looked on covetously by passersby, they were also trampled and knocked into like passengers on the aisle seats of an aeroplane.

The plaza is framed by white Andalusian buildings, the most illustrious of which is the city hall. In a repeat of scenes I had observed across the country, three flags proudly adorned the building's balcony: the flag of the local autonomous community (in this case the green and white of Andalucia), the Spanish flag, and the flag of the Europe Union. Even before Brexit you would never have seen similar displays on municipal buildings in Britain. I was amazed to learn Britain even had regional flags. While the Andalusian flag has been proudly flown for more than a century, it is only within the last decade that there has been a belated push for Britain's counties to, as it were, fly the flag. I looked up some I might recognise, but to no avail. For example, Surrey, where I spent my childhood, is represented by a giant yellow and blue chessboard. I've no idea why.

Walking through the narrow streets nearby, I passed countless boutique shops until I reached the Plaza de la Iglesia, which is, as you may expect, dominated by a church. Just as with the cathedral in Granada, the church of Santa María de la Encarnación was built on what had previously been the location of Marbella's largest mosque. A stone's throw away, marking the eastern edge of the old town, is the ruins of the city's 11th century castle.

I began looking for a place to eat dinner. Of course, there were plenty of restaurants to choose from, but none I could afford. It reminded me of the lines from Samuel Taylor Coleridge's poem *The Rime of the Ancient Mariner*:

Water, water, everywhere,
Nor any drop to drink.

Even down-at-heel restaurants with faded facades were expensive. Marbella's reputation evidently brought with it significant price inflation. Cheap and cheerful Fuengirola was much more my style. I amused myself by examining the cost of the dishes at some of the fancier establishments. Obviously, some didn't include prices at all (why would you let an irrelevant factor such as cost influence where you ate?) but the prices of those that did were eye-watering. The customers arriving in these places were dressed up to the nines, with several of the women wearing ball gowns. They were in Marbella and were intent on making sure they were seen there.

I could no longer ignore my rumbling stomach and I settled upon a Chinese restaurant by a roundabout a few streets away. It may not have aided my understanding of Spanish culture, but their buffet was just what I needed.

Spared from spending €10 on two miniscule cheese croquettes, I contented myself with demolishing platefuls of greasy fat masquerading as meat. This time none of the waiters felt compelled to tell me how handsome I was, but I put that down to the fact they watched me gorge on every dish in sight for two hours. Feeling the size of a house, I eventually left and shuffled through the twilight up the hill towards my Airbnb accommodation.

I was greeted by Hugo, a friendly thirty-something with an elaborate blond quiff. I stayed in Marbella for two nights and made the most of my last rest day on the coast before I reached Gibraltar. I had enjoyed the easy days of cycling between seaside resorts since I had escaped the Sierras de Tejeda, Almijara y Alhama Natural Park, but it was time to head back inland. Picturesque Ronda beckoned - and a hard day in the saddle lay in store.

25

Marbella to Ronda

Before the pain came the beauty. I cycled along the seafront in the early morning sun, with no one around except for a few eager runners. The restaurants lining the route soon disappeared, leaving only palm trees along Marbella's Golden Mile. More a marketing ploy than a geographic description, the 'mile' covers a 6.4km stretch of sandy beaches that run all the way to the town of Puerto Banús. Created by José Banús, a local property developer who just so happened to be close friends with Franco, the resort opened to much fanfare in 1970. Guests at the launch party included Prince Rainier of Monaco, the future king of Spain Juan Carlos I, the film director Roman Polanski and Playboy founder Hugh Hefner. More than 22kg of caviar was provided for what must have been quite the party. Puerto Banús has carried on in much the same vein ever since. It continues to thrive and has successfully portrayed itself as a playground for the rich and famous.

It's unclear how long this will remain the case. One restaurant owner recently commented, 'Now what we get are people wearing Liverpool and Manchester United shirts. Puerto Banús is not what it was.'

As I cycled west along the Golden Mile, small waves lapped gently onto the sand to my left. On my right-hand side, a series of high walls and hedges carefully concealed properties built on one of the most expensive strips of real estate in the country. King Fahd of Saudi Arabia had a place constructed here, on land which is now worth an estimated £120m.

Shortly after passing the hundreds of yachts gleaming in the sunshine at the harbour of Puerto Banús, I turned away from the shore towards Ronda. To get there, I needed to travel north on a single A-road for nearly 50km. In an attempt to avoid the road and the traffic leaving Puerto Banús for as long as possible, I took a diversion via a few high-end apartment complexes built on the hillside. The map indicated there was a single junction where I could later rejoin the road. However, in the web of dead-end streets and manicured gardens, I quickly strayed off course. As the heat intensified, my frustration grew, for I was aware of the knock-on effect the delay would have when I finally began the climb to Ronda. Belatedly, I found the steep road that would lead me out of the complex and began slowly cycling up towards the main road. Just as I was hoping to see the exit, I was met by the far less welcome sight of a locked gate with an accompanying sign warning that trespassers would be prosecuted.

I thought about taking my chances, but the gate was too high to hurriedly throw my bike over the top. More to the point, there were several CCTV cameras looking straight at me, so even if I managed it, I wouldn't get very far before being escorted off the premises. Exasperated and drenched in sweat, I waited a little while to see if a kind soul would let me in. No one came. I was loath to return to Puerto Banús, and scoured the map for another option. I found it in a small left turn approximately 50 metres back that briefly ran alongside the main road.

Rarely has anyone been so pleased to see rubbish-strewn, forgotten scrubland. From my shortcut, the only impediments to reaching the main road was a collapsed wire fence and the roadside barrier. I bounded over the first before lifting my bike over the railing and carefully placing it on the hard shoulder. The traffic wasn't as heavy as I had feared, but I could feel the gusts of dusty air on my face as the vehicles drove past. And although the gradient of the road looked severe, at that moment I didn't care. I was out of the maze and back on course towards Ronda, on a route that, according to the website andalucia.com, 'has a deserved reputation for excitement and danger'.

The climb seemed endless and the number of places to pull over for a rest were few and far between. I marvelled at the fitness of the cyclists in the Tour de France and craved the supply of food and drink the riders receive from support staff in the team cars. A rare roadside viewpoint looked over the neighbouring mountains of the Sierra Palmitera and down towards the Mediterranean far below. It deserved a name befitting its panoramic views, but it was simply called A-397 Lookout. With a name like that, I doubted it featured in many guidebooks, but it was satisfying to see the progress I had made since I left Puerto Banús' sheltered shoreline.

The ascent was taking a heavy toll on my legs and I was getting worryingly low on water. Just as I was calculating how long I could make it last, I spotted a fortuitously located natural spring up ahead. My eyes were drawn to it by the sight of two men filling five of the 20-litre bottles you see fitted onto water coolers in offices. I stopped next to them to wait my turn. The exertion of the previous hour must have been etched across my face because the men, who were both in their sixties, immediately stepped back to allow me to fill my own water bottles.

'*¿Desde dónde has venido?*' one of them asked. Where have you come from?

'*Salí de Marbella esta mañana,*' I answered with as casual a shrug as I could manage as I tried to downplay the enormous effort I had expended since I had departed Marbella.

The two men looked at their car and beyond to the sea on the horizon behind it. They laughed as if I was mad. It would have been hard to argue with them; I hadn't seen anyone else crazy enough to cycle up or down this route.

I glugged the delicious fresh water and the men resumed filling their bottles. They were curious to know where I was heading.

'Ronda,' I replied breathlessly. The men laughed again.

When the bottles were full one of the men picked one up, staggering as he carried it over the road to the car.

Upon witnessing his struggles, the other man began rolling a bottle across the ground. The bottle's shape prevented it from running true, and he was soon zigzagging across the road as the bottle veered off at irregular angles.

'*¿Puedo ayudarle a llevar la botella?*' I asked. I would have been quicker to offer assistance carrying the bottle if I didn't find the sentence structure of such questions quite so challenging. Caught up in the moment, it's easy to get verb conjugations mixed up so that instead of offering a hand to someone in need, you end up asking for them to help you.

'*No,*' the man replied puffing. '*¡Para donde vas, necesitarás mucha energía!*' Where you're going, you will need your energy!

I laughed nervously as I refilled my water bottle and reflected on how experiences such as this, where I was chatting in Spanish to strangers by mountain springs, was exactly what I had hoped for when I left Valencia.

I was shaken from my reverie by the unexpected sound of throaty engine noises. Startled, the three of us couldn't see what was creating the noise further down the mountain, but the man rolling the bottle wasn't hanging around to be flattened as he found out, and he hastily made his way to the safety of the roadside. I had come across numerous groups of motorcyclists over the past few weeks, who, like me, were out to enjoy the exhilarating mountain passes and irresistible coastal roads. So I knew these engine roars weren't coming from motorbikes. I've also watched enough episodes of *Top Gear* to recognise that the sound didn't belong to a convoy of supercars. As the sound grew louder, the three of us craned our necks to see 20 go-karts driving up the road towards us in a scene straight out of *Mario Kart*. The drivers genially waved at our bemused faces as they went past.

Looking out for banana skins and oil slicks, I carried on riding for half an hour until I came to a restaurant at a bend in the road. I knew it would almost certainly be the last place serving food this side of Ronda. A lone trucker was seated on one of the plastic chairs under the parapet and he eyed me with curiosity as I locked my bike. Inside, the restaurant was empty except for a bored barmaid.

'*Buenas tardes,*' I said cheerfully. '*¿Puedo ver la carta?*'

The barmaid looked aghast at my request to see the menu. '*Tendrá que esperar, el cocinero está demasiado ocupado en este momento.*' You will have to wait - the chef is too busy right now.'

I looked around. '*Pero, no hay nadie más aquí...*' But there isn't anyone else here...

'*No, pero si llega alguien más, el cocinero no podrá preparar tantos pedidos al mismo tiempo.*' No, but if someone else arrives, the chef won't be able to prepare so many orders at the same time. The barmaid was apparently unaware that down on the coast many restaurants achieved such a feat every day. '*Cuando sirva la comida al hombre que está afuera, puede entrar y hacer su pedido.*' When the food is served to the man outside, you can come in and order your food then. She said this with such straightforward matter-of-factness, I was at a loss to argue.

While I waited, I tried to guess what kind of fine cuisine the chef in this dusty joint would be conjuring up. The answer, it transpired, was egg and chips. To keep things simple, I ordered chips and turned my attention to the view as I waited for the food to come out of the microwave. I could no longer see the Mediterranean, which was now hidden behind the mountains. Looking back over the way I had come, I could follow the road snaking around the hillside and tried, without success, to trace the journey ahead. The only thing I could tell was that there was no sign of the summit.

When I went back in to pay, the sourpuss barmaid refused to refill my rapidly emptying water bottle from the tap and tried to charge me a small fortune for a bottle that scarcely contained enough water to wet my lips. I paid for the chips and walked out in barely disguised disgust. The trucker must have overheard the conversation, for he pointed me in the direction of a tap around the back of the building that supplied clean water and was used to hose down dusty vehicles travelling to Puerto Banús. I thanked him, hoping the water was as hygienic as he claimed.

Higher up the mountain, I was soon so thirsty I ceased worrying about the potability of the water. The gradient had flattened a little, but the road kept climbing ever higher, draining my energy in the fierce heat. I was cheered considerably when I saw two mountain goats standing by the roadside. Up to that point this leg of the journey had been far from one of my favourites - it was too much hard work for that - but I acknowledged it wasn't every day that you get to pass both sandy beaches and mountain goats on the same bike ride.

A little further on I reached Igualeja Viewpoint. The spot was marked by a two-pronged, seven-metre tall rust coloured sculpture dedicated to the little known Bohemian-Austrian poet Rainer Maria Rilke. No other information was provided about him. I discovered online that Rilke is regarded as one of the most lyrically intense and mystical of the German-language poets. Which does sound rather like the prize for the tallest dwarf. He's honoured on a hill on the outskirts of Ronda because he spent several months in the municipality at the start of the 20th century, describing it as 'the city of his dreams'. The fact that a local road improvement company's attempts to find a use for its surplus steel coincided with the creation of the monument is, of course, completely unrelated. The sculpture, now sadly daubed with graffiti, stands next to the unfinished concrete shell of a visitor centre optimistically commissioned during more economically prosperous times. Combined, the two structures looked less like a celebration of the surrounding stunning scenery, and more like the desolate debris left behind by the explosion of an atomic bomb.

At the lookout a sign stated I was now 1,130 metres above sea level. This made the ascent a little shorter than my earlier efforts in the Sierra Nevada. The following month the Tour de France was held, featuring eight climbs of more than 1,000 metres, some of which were on the same day. While the professionals obviously don't carry 11kg of kit and aren't using bikes that weigh the same again, I didn't fancy my chances of climbing another kilometre that afternoon. Thankfully, I didn't need to - the lookout marked the highest point of the day.

Initially, the descent was so gradual that a passenger in a car would have been unlikely to notice the difference to the incremental incline of a few hundred metres before. While almost imperceptible in a vehicle, such a change makes a substantial difference on a bicycle. What had previously been a psychological trial of mental strength was transformed into a carefree cruise. The weight of my pannier bags, for so long a millstone around my neck, gathered momentum as I freewheeled through the foothills of the Sierra de las Nieves Natural Park and the farmland south-east of Ronda. It was getting on towards 3pm and only now were a few clouds beginning to dot the sky. Never one to count my chickens, I anticipated the journey might have a sting in the tail, but now I was the other side of the mountains I made good progress and within an hour saw a mass of whitewashed buildings appear on the horizon.

Not long after, I rolled into Ronda, arriving at the Almocábar Gate which marks the southern entrance to the city. I say city, but it's hard to pinpoint exactly what kind of place Ronda is. Depending where you look, it's variously described as a village, a town or a city. Given it has a population of fewer than 34,000 people, its city status, bestowed during the time of Julius Caesar, feels a little inappropriate today. At any rate, it remains one of Spain's most popular destinations and the 'city' walls contain more history than a multitude of metropolises.

I sat in the shade of the plaza next to the Almocábar Gate, eating a celebratory orange as I admired its imposing twin towers. I didn't stay long because I was impatient to see Ronda's iconic bridge. It was the reason Ronda was one of the first places I wrote down when planning my route across the country four years previously during breaks on late night shifts at Sky News. The bridge spans the Tajo Gorge and is supported by two long legs of stone that descend 100 metres to the riverbank. Just like the Alhambra in Granada, the attraction is instantly recognisable and provided plentiful motivation to travel inland and conquer the mountains in order to discover.

Ronda could only fail to live up to my sky-high expectations. And yet I fell in love with it immediately as I cycled through the narrow streets towards the bridge. Referred to as the New Bridge, it is of course not new at all, having been constructed towards the end of the 18th century. Although the bridge is wide enough for a car, it receives only limited traffic as residents sensibly steer clear of the area to avoid congestion. So as I approached the bridge I was met, not by an oncoming car, but by a horse-drawn carriage trotting towards me. Aimed exclusively at tourists, I'd normally have judged this to be terribly twee, but as I shut my eyes and listened to its hooves clopping against the cobblestones, I felt I had been transported back in time.

Peering over the bridge, I followed the vertical rock face down to the water below. Unable to help myself, I recalled reading that the first bridge to span this part of the gorge had collapsed, plunging 50 people to their deaths. Instinctively raising my gaze, I could see shadows forming on the contours of the hillsides and local farmland. To the east, the Sierra de las Nieves Natural Park loomed in the distance, while on the other side of the bridge, the peaks of the Sierra de Grazalema Natural Park towered over the golden countryside.

Reluctantly, I decided to wait until the following day to walk down into the gorge to see the bridge from its most famous angle. The pace of life was noticeably slower in Ronda and the city felt a million miles away from the glitz and glamour of the nouveau riche in Marbella and Puerto Banús. Of course, there were groups of tourists milling around, but the crowds dissipated as the afternoon wore on and day-trippers were soon filing onto the buses to head back to their hotels in Malaga, Granada and Seville.

As evening approached I ventured across the bridge to the northern district of Ronda, where I ate dinner and then met my softly spoken Airbnb host, Leonardo. An elderly man with an immaculate silver moustache, he lived alone in a spacious apartment. The steps up to it were lined with carefully tended pot plants and, inside, the spotless living room was filled with framed photos of his sons and daughters, nieces and nephews. Yet he seemed lonely.

I asked him about his family and his recommendations for my time in Ronda. We talked for a while and he spoke lovingly about his wife who had died a couple of years previously. It was nice for a change to spend time with someone who wasn't hosting me for the meagre money I was bringing to the table, but for the conversation I might provide. Now more than a month into my trip, the companionship was mutually beneficial.

26

Ronda

A lot was expected of Pedro Romero. Born in Ronda into a dynasty of bullfighters, his family had changed the game. In 1726 his grandfather, Francisco, became the first man to fight the bull on foot; all previous combatants in Spain had been mounted on horses. Furthermore, he popularised the *muleta*, the cloak that draws the bull's attention, and redesigned it so that it was connected to a concealed stick. Pedro's father, Juan, was the first to use a team of bullfighters to orchestrate the fight. Juan was handsomely rewarded for his innovation, but it came at a high personal cost. His eldest son and Pedro's brother, Gaspar, was killed during a fight while working as one of his assistants. His youngest son was also later gored to death. What could little Pedro bring to the table? And would he stay alive long enough to deliver it? As it turns out, he outdid them all.

While not as innovative as his forebears, he is considered the first matador to truly conceive of the bullfight as an art and a skill in its own right. He killed an estimated 5,600 bulls over the course of his career without suffering an injury. This is in spite of the fact that he was still being brought out of retirement in his late seventies. A statue of Pedro Romero now stands near the entrance of Ronda's prettiest park, Alameda del Tajo.

It was here that I ate breakfast. Sunlight had streamed through the curtains of my room so I was up early and able to appreciate the tranquility of the park before the crowds arrived. The only people there were locals walking their dogs or wrinkly old men whose skin had been aged by decades of sun exposure and cigarettes. They sat apart, smoking on the benches. An attractive tree-lined avenue ran down the centre of the park and the dense foliage of the canopy provided both shade and a framing device for the view of the mountains of the Sierra de Grazalema Natural Park. At the end of the avenue was the lip of the gorge. Averting my eyes from the morning sun, I looked down towards the dusty road that connected the houses dotted around far below and admired their outdoor swimming pools.

As I turned to stroll back through the park, I noticed an elderly man with thinning dyed black hair listening to a huge radio that must have been at least 40 years old. I slowed as I approached to see how much I could understand of the broadcast. To my disappointment, it wasn't much. I smiled a non-committal good morning to the man, who surprised me by engaging me in conversation. I enjoyed practising my Spanish as he told me about his life, but I lost interest when he kept repeating the same gibberish about Jews.

Next door to the park is the city's famous bullring. Only one fight takes place there a year now, as part of the annual Pedro Romero Festival. The bullring, and its complementary museum, is one of Ronda's most popular tourist attractions. Yet I had deep misgivings about visiting it. I didn't doubt I would find it interesting, but paying money in support of such a cruel activity was, to my mind, ethically unjustifiable. Taunting and then repeatedly stabbing a bull to death is a strange way to celebrate artistry and courage.

In Portugal, one of the few places around the world other than Spain where bullfighting is still tolerated, the spectacle is perceived to be more civilised because the animals are not killed in view of the public. Entertainment that is derived from provoking a bull into charging and then carting him off to be killed in private by a butcher is a pretty low bar for acceptability though. I'm no vegan, so I accept I'm hardly a paragon of virtue, but I elected to show my distaste by voting with my feet.

Travel often throws up ethical dilemmas such as this. More than a decade ago I was offered the opportunity to watch a cockfight in Nicaragua. I accepted in haste and have repented at leisure ever since. The poor birds, armed with small knives tied to their feet, were provoked into attacking each other. A baying crowd of gamblers encircled the pit where the roosters were fighting and blood soon splattered their plumage. The fights only ended when one cock was lying on the ground quivering in pain and immobilised. Of course, the owners of each bird could have stopped the violence by conceding defeat and waving a dirty dish cloth someone had brought with them. However, unlike boxing trainers who (usually) care about their fighter's wellbeing, the owners of the cocks weren't too concerned whether their competitor was served for dinner that night or another. They simply wanted to win.

When presented with another travel dilemma, whether to climb up Uluru (Ayers Rock), a few months later, I declined. Aboriginal Australians have asked people not to do so for decades as the landmark is sacred in their culture. The route has now been permanently closed. Nonetheless, I don't regret my decision. And nor, when I'm grey and old, do I think I will rue missing out on visiting Spain's oldest bullring.

Pedro Romero may be Ronda's most lauded former inhabitant, but my vote goes to Abbas Ibn Firnas. Born in Ronda in the 9th century, Ibn Firnas was a mercurial polymath: an inventor, physician, chemist, engineer, musician and poet. In a crowded field, it is arguably his achievements in aviation that were the most groundbreaking. He is credited for developing the world's first parachute and proved his invention worked by voluntarily jumping from the tower of Cordoba's mosque. Talk about backing yourself. He broke some bones upon landing, but was unbowed and went on to design the first ever wingsuit. Again, Ibn Firnas demonstrated its effectiveness himself, attaching silk and feathers to his body before running down a hill to briefly become airborne. His legacy has been recognised with a statue outside Baghdad International Airport and the naming of a crater on the moon in his honour. A double that eluded even Saddam Hussein.

From the bullring I walked across the city and down into the Tajo Gorge. I couldn't take my eyes off the bridge, which wasn't ideal as the stone pathing abruptly gave way to a dusty footpath of jagged rocks. As I descended, I could see a small waterfall as the Guadalevín river flowed into a concealed pool below. The cascade probably wasn't actually small at all, but was inevitably dwarfed by the bridge's immense stone pillars that towered either side of it. During the Spanish Civil War, both sides are alleged to have killed prisoners by throwing them off the bridge. Accounts of these events are believed to have informed Ernest Hemingway's book *For Whom The Bell Tolls*.

Ronda's residents fiercely opposed Franco's Nationalist forces and local guerrilla groups formed when the Nationalists seized control of the city. The rebels lived as bandits in the neighbouring mountains for several years and remained there when the war was over. Even as late as 1952, buses travelling through the Serranía de Ronda were accompanied by the military to secure their safe passage.

I eventually dragged myself away from staring at the bridge and walked back into town to explore the House of the Moorish King. The name is a complete misnomer as the house was built in the 18th century, long after the Moorish kings had all been vanquished. Yet the house does incorporate one important relic of Ronda's Moorish era: the Water Mine. Not knowing what to expect, I walked down a long, cramped, dank staircase carved into the walls of the cliff. I hit my head multiple times on the low ceiling and was beginning to doubt whether it was going to be worth the hassle, when I emerged at the bottom of the gorge to a scene of beautiful serenity.

An area the size of a small patio overlooked the crystal-clear blue water gently making its way towards the New Bridge. Far from just an attractive cove, this secret inlet was of critical importance during episodes in Ronda's history. The city's geographic attributes long made it impervious to attack, so invading armies tried to force the inhabitants to surrender by cutting off their water supply. On such occasions, the mine kept the population alive. In the 15th century the Christian army was similarly thwarted until its leaders learned, allegedly from a Muslim traitor, how residents were continuing to access water when all the known supply lines had been cut. The Christians duly attacked the site, destroying the concealed water mill at the bottom of the mine. The population began to die of dehydration and the city fell days later.

I headed back into the darkness and up the slippery stairs, feeling the unpleasant, cold, clammy sensation on my arms and back as I was pressed against the damp wall by people squeezing past me in the opposite direction. Michelle Obama visited the mine during her time as First Lady, but I doubt she had the same experience. Drying off in the sunlight, I walked across the less heralded Old Bridge, which has existed, in one form or another, since the 16th century. Just across the bridge, on the opposite side of the gorge to the House of the Moorish King, are the Cuenca Gardens. The tiered park was built on the edge of the gorge and was full of roses in bloom. I was amazed to find I had it all to myself. Happily seated at the top of the gardens, I enjoyed an astounding view of the opposite side of the New Bridge to the one I'd seen earlier that day.

I rounded off the afternoon with an ice cream. Not just any ice cream, you understand, but one so special it made my eyes widen and my pupils dilate the instant I tasted it on my tongue. You can have a thousand ice creams in a lifetime - I intend to - but only some will stay with you forever. Some you'll remember for the wrong reasons, such as when you're a child and the ice cream falls to the ground at your feet. Luckily, this wasn't one of those moments.

Sarah, I knew, would always opt for chocolate ice cream, but I know the correct flavour to choose at any one moment should depend on an infinitely complex range of factors such as how hot the weather is, how thirsty someone is and the type of cone on offer. The only exception to this rule is a Pooh Bear. If offered, always have a Pooh Bear. What's a Pooh Bear I hear you ask? Part of the ice cream's appeal is its mystique, but as far as I can gather it's a mixture of crunchy honeycomb, vanilla and caramel. I was only aware of one place where you could buy this delicacy; in Bangor, the seaside town where my mum grew up in Northern Ireland.

This all changed that afternoon in Ronda.

Upon tasting the ice cream, I was transported straight from sunny Spain to cloudy County Down. It's not a well-trodden route, I'll admit, but I was thrilled. To my shame, I can't remember the Spanish name for the ice cream, so you'll have to go to Bangor to try it. Anyway, Northern Ireland's tourist board needs you more than Ronda's.

216

That evening was the first match of real significance of the 2018 FIFA World Cup. Spain were playing Portugal and the match was billed as the defending world champions versus Real Madrid's Portuguese star striker Cristiano Ronaldo. I anticipated the city's bars would be a great place to watch the match, but although a few local men sat down at the tables nearby when the game was under way, it was far from the feverish atmosphere I'd expected. The match itself did live up to the hype though, with Ronaldo scoring a hat-trick in a thrilling 3-3 draw.

27

Ronda to Alcalá de los Gazules

I began the day with the target of cycling 151km to Tarifa, the southernmost point of mainland Europe. This distance was considerably further than I had cycled in a single day before, but I reasoned that as much of the journey would be downhill, I'd make it if I started early. The route passed through two national parks that cut a swathe of green right across the map, beginning just west of Ronda and running all the way to the coast. It was to be the final push; the last long day on the bike before I was back riding along the shore. I was already eyeing up the possibility of hiring a surfboard in Tarifa.

Sadly, these aspirations did not come to pass.

I set off early with the best of intentions and left Ronda's suburbs behind me as I cycled through fields of wheat illuminated gold by the rising sun. I was enjoying the stillness of the morning air and feeling good when I found myself at the bottom of a long, steep hill below the village of Benaoján. My calves begged for mercy as I grunted my way up to the traditional Andalusian-style houses built on the plateau above. I stopped briefly in Benaoján to recover while eating an orange, before resuming the gently winding ascent out of the village. It was only from afar that the beauty of Benaoján's setting was revealed. What before had seemed another nice, if unremarkable, village of classic white buildings, now shone like a jewel. Ensconced by towering, jagged peaks, it looked like a latter-day Machu Picchu.

I kept cycling uphill and was soon level with the top of the adjacent mountains. The single-track road meandered around rocky outcrops and was only just wide enough for vehicles. I rarely came across cars, but when I did, drivers routinely pulled over to let me pass. As a show of thanks, I'd respond by increasing my cadence so the driver wouldn't need to wait for long. One jovial driver in his sixties acknowledged my efforts by impersonating me, puffing hard as he mimicked my peddling by comically rotating his fists in front of his chest. I smiled in acknowledgment of his good-natured teasing. He obviously wasn't in a rush. In my experience, it doesn't matter which country you're in, the stereotype of people who live in the countryside being friendlier than the average city slicker rings true. You don't get that kind of gentle humour when you're commuting across London.

The journey through the Sierra de Grazalema was a

cyclist's dream; no hill too hard, but not so flat as to be dull. And just as the temperature began to intensify in the late morning, I entered an area of woodland providing welcome shade. Occasionally, snatched glimpses of the vast open plain below would emerge between the trees. It was like a cross between cycling alone on a sunny day in Richmond Park in London and stumbling into *The Land That Time Forgot*. This may be a puzzling reference as, admittedly, I didn't see any dinosaurs. Moreover, it is, of course, impossible to cycle alone on a sunny day in Richmond Park, due to the constant stream of lycra-clad men around every bend. Just like in sections of the park though, dappled sunlight streamed through the canopy of surrounding oak trees onto the winding narrow road.

I made a similar improbable observation when I visited the Tierra del Fuego archipelago at the southern tip of South America. I had long been excited to see what wild landscape awaited me in this 'land of fire' and was disappointed to find it was all quite familiar. Despite being the starting point for trips to Antarctica, the region is a similar distance from the equator as southern England. So while my imagination pictured a fiery Mount Doom from *The Lord of the Rings*, I arrived at the national park to find the same muddy paths and beech trees that I had spent my childhood among. Different, but the same.

Even so, there was something unusual about the oak trees of the Sierra de Grazalema. They had all been stripped of their bark to just above head height, exposing the red timber beneath. Shorn of their outer layer, the red trees appeared embarrassed by their nakedness. I attributed this to a forest fire, but I knew this didn't make sense as there were no tell-tale signs of the flames licking up the sides of the trees, only a uniform height up to where the bark of all the trees had been removed. It was more like the trunks showed the high water mark of where a toxic, bark-dissolving flood had swept across the land.

Inevitably, the truth is more prosaic. These trees were cork oak trees and their red colour suggested they had been stripped within the last fortnight. Stripping only takes place once a decade so I was lucky to see such an arresting sight. The bark will slowly regenerate using the carbon stored in the trees and each tree can be expected to produce one tonne of raw cork during its lifetime: the equivalent of 65,000 cork stops.

Anyone with even a passing interest in cycling should visit this stunning stretch of countryside. It was no surprise to learn that four years earlier these narrow roads had hosted Spain's most prestigious race, the Vuelta a España, which sits alongside the Giro d'Italia and the Tour de France as one of the three Grand Tours of European cycling.

I smiled with giddy excitement as I navigated each turn in the road. After all the climbs of the past month, it seemed too good to last.

It was.

As I emerged from the wooded hillside onto the sunny plain below, along a road that seemed to run into the distance forever, my broken spoke came loose from its position, contorted around another spoke and snapped it off. Bizarrely, the thought that came to mind was a scene from the movie *Apollo 13*. When an engine briefly cuts out during take-off, Tom Hanks' Jim Lovell says to his crewmates, 'Looks like we've had our glitch for this mission'. I consoled myself with this sentiment. Unfortunately, just as was the case for Tom, more serious problems lay ahead. I was out of the woods in only a literal sense.

I stopped briefly at a viewpoint located where the Sierra de Grazalema in the north and the southerly Los Alcornocales Natural Park converge. In a nearby empty bar that I was shocked to find open, I bought a bottle of water. I was glad I did; there was only one other place selling drinks in the 42km that followed. That was a small, ramshackle restaurant built on a junction, 20km down the road. The owner there kindly refilled my water and I sat outside on the gravel which served, optimistically, as a customer car park. I had hoped to have lunch at Alcalá de los Gazules, but it was already 1pm and I still had a long way to go. Reluctantly, I accepted that I'd need to eat before I reached the town. I continued cycling but, unable to find a pleasant spot for lunch, I eventually conceded defeat and collapsed onto a bundle of weeds by the roadside. Within minutes, ants had gathered around my banana skin, while mosquitos, thankfully absent for the majority of the trip, swarmed around my sweaty body. Hot and bothered, but at least no longer hungry, I pushed on again.

There was no longer any shade, but the descent towards Alcalá de los Gazules was marvellous. No one was in sight and I could let my mind wander as I listened to the noise of the crickets in the bushes.

The town of Alcalá de los Gazules sits at the summit of a vertiginous hill that rises from the valley floor. As I rode towards the white buildings above me, I cursed the settlers of bygone days for having the wisdom to build their homes in places that were so difficult to attack.

I picked up my first puncture as I pulled into the town. After all these weeks and all of the unsuitable terrain I'd travelled across, I'd begun to believe that, maybe, just maybe, I might make it to Gibraltar with my inner tubes intact. To my dismay, when I emptied my panniers to turn my bike upside down, I realised my predicament was worse than I had first assumed. The bike didn't have a quick release mechanism to separate the wheel from the frame. Much like electric windows in the front of cars, I'd assumed that all new bikes, no matter how low budget, were now fitted with these. I was wrong.

In place of where I expected to see the quick release lever was a very solid looking nut and screw that required a spanner to loosen. I had a basic bike kit with me, but, to my shame, it didn't have a spanner. I'd like to pretend this was a deliberate decision taken to reduce the weight I was carrying, but in reality it was simply a massive oversight. It was mid-afternoon on a Saturday and almost all of the shops in the largely deserted town square were closed. It didn't look like I would be leaving Alcalá de los Gazules any time soon.

I walked around trying to find some signs of life. At the far corner of a plaza I found a bar, and after hastily looking up the translation for 'spanner', I stepped inside. The bar was empty except for a pensioner talking to a young barman who was wearing a figure-hugging black t-shirt. While I waited for their conversation to draw to a close, I watched a bullfight being broadcast on the brown cube of an old television hanging from the corner of the ceiling. Like motorway drivers unable to resist slowing down to look at a crash, I couldn't help watching on with interest. As the customer walked outside, the barman turned to me.

'*Buenas tardes. ¿Tiene una llave por favor?*' I asked hopefully.

He looked at me quizzically, unsure if I'd intended to say those words. The question was particularly ambiguous because the word for spanner, *una llave*, is much more commonly used to refer to a key. Even if the barman correctly guessed I was seeking a spanner rather than a key, I knew there was a high chance he would simply laugh in my face before responding, 'A spanner? Why on Earth would I have a spanner?' If he had, I wouldn't have blamed him.

Giving my Spanish the benefit of the doubt, he ruminated for a little while on where such a tool might be kept. Delighted not to have been dismissed out of hand, I watched as he began rummaging through some drawers.

'Ah ha!' he exclaimed, brandishing a spanner as if it was the sword in the stone. He handed it to me and I almost bowed in gratitude.

However, try as I might, I couldn't loosen the nut. I must have looked pretty pathetic because as I paused to summon my strength again, a motorcyclist with skin even more weathered than his worn out black leather riding trousers took pity on me. I tried to explain the issue in my limited bike Spanish, but he waved my words away as he turned his attention to the nut. To my amazement, he managed to unfasten it. Normally, I'd have felt humiliated by this turn of events, but my overriding emotion was that of relief. I thanked him repeatedly and insisted on buying both him and the barman a drink. The barman chose a beer while the motorcyclist opted for a double shot of vodka. He downed the drink without a word, walked back to his bike and rode off into the distance. I, meanwhile, returned to my bike. I wasn't in the mindset to repair the inner tube, so I replaced it with my spare one and put the wheel back on the bike.

Something wasn't right though. As I tested the new inner tube, my derailleur (the mechanism used to move the chain from one cog to the next when changing gear) hit the spokes of my rear wheel in every one but the highest gear. Considering their already fragile state, this was the last thing the spokes needed. After studying my rear wheel, the gearing and comparative images on Google, I concluded that my derailleur was irrevocably bent out of shape. I still have no idea how it happened. I can only think the weight of the bags on one side of my pannier rack must have knocked it.

To avoid looking like a cartoon character, peddling frantically in order to move anywhere, it was far better to be stuck in the highest gear than having to rely solely on the lowest. Nevertheless, while it was downhill the majority of the way to Tarifa, I didn't fancy my chances of tackling any remaining inclines with the current setup. But it appeared I wouldn't have much choice.

By now it was 5pm. I had started the day with such lofty ambitions, but they were now fizzling out before my eyes. There was no way I was getting to Tarifa before nightfall. Even I had the sense to accept that attempting to complete the final 62km on a crippled bike with only one gear, no spare inner tube and without any daylight for many of the remaining kilometres was beyond stupid. It was hardly wise to try it the next day, but I'd have to take my chances. I could, of course, have ditched the bike and jumped on a bus, but a brief glance of the timetable at the town's only bus stop confirmed that there wasn't a Sunday service, meaning I could walk to Tarifa in the time it took for the next bus to turn up.

I'd intended to find a hostel when I reached Tarifa, so at least this time no one was awaiting my arrival. To shorten the next day's journey, I contemplated limping 20km further south that evening to the next town along, Benalup-Casas Viejas, but decided it wasn't worth the risk of failing to find a place to sleep there. So, feeling like the Virgin Mary on Christmas Eve, I began searching for accommodation in Alcalá de los Gazules. Short on options, I accepted a room above a bar which looked like it was straight off the set of a horror movie. There were holes in the sink, stains in the toilet and blood on the sheets. I was glad to have brought my sleeping bag liner.

I went back outside to spend another hour trying to fix my bike. Devoid of ideas, I eventually gave up and endeavoured to make the most of my time in Alcalá de los Gazules. One of Spain's most celebrated poets, Federico García Lorca, described the town as 'intimately Andaluz' and, although I was in a sour mood for a while, the whitewashed buildings were undeniably beautiful in the golden light of the evening sun.

Returning to the bar underneath my room, I ate dinner while nursing a beer in front of another World Cup match. The day had been both physically and mentally draining, so at the final whistle I went upstairs to bed, hoping that luck would be with me the following day. I would need it.

28

Alcalá de los Gazules to Tarifa

Having to cycle in the bike's highest gear was far from ideal, but I was more preoccupied by the possibility of picking up another puncture. The villages appeared to be even more remote on the road to Tarifa than they had been approaching Alcalá de los Gazules. Even though I had been tired and stressed the night before, I regretted not having attempted to mend the damaged inner tube. Now that I'd used my spare, if I did get a puncture I'd have no choice but to repair it. The usual way of doing this is to find the (often miniscule) hole in the tube by sticking it in water to see where the bubbles emerge. But with no sources of water in the dry grassland of the countryside around me, locating a puncture would be no easy task.

I unsuccessfully tried to find an inner tube in Benalup-Casas Viejas, where the only place open early on a Sunday morning was the petrol station. Sunday lie-ins undoubtedly contributed to the town's sleepy appearance, but I suspected Benalup-Casas Viejas was little different during the working week.

As hard as it was to believe, it was a hotbed of political activity in the 1930s however, when oppressed agricultural workers repeatedly turned to violence to demand wage increases. After orchestrating a local rebellion, a small group of militants tried to resist arrest in 1933 by barricading themselves and their families in the cottage of local anarchist Francisco 'Six Fingers' Cruz Gutiérrez. The police responded by setting the building alight and it burned down with everyone inside. Officers then arrested anyone in the village who possessed a gun, marched them to the smoking ashes of their dead neighbours and shot them in the back. In total 24 people died. When reports of the incident began to circulate, they sparked national outrage, which eroded support for the nascent Spanish Second Republic and led Benalup-Casas Viejas to become a revolutionary symbol for the anarchist movement across Spain.

On the other side of town I was faced with a decision. Either I could take an off-road shortcut along unknown terrain to trim 33km off the journey, or I could stay on the relative safety of the asphalt for 60km until I reached the village of Facinas. Hoping that fortune would favour the brave, I gambled on the shorter route. From the junction the track had looked relatively well maintained, but it swiftly deteriorated a little more than a kilometre further on and I was soon cycling through dried mud fields full of nonplussed cows and desiccated dung. The path continued to disintegrate and, before long, it was too rough to ride, so I walked with my wounded bike for a couple of hours through vast undulating wheat fields.

Approaching the brow of another dusty hill, I heard a deep, resonant whirring sound I couldn't place. Its origin was revealed from the summit; around 30 wind turbines, all moving at an impressive pace either side of the path ahead. Beyond them was the gratifying sight of a sprawl of white houses built on the facing hillside. Appearing like an oasis in the desert, Facinas was the first sign of civilization I had encountered since I left Benalup-Casas Viejas. As I passed underneath the gigantic gleaming white poles of the towering turbines, the rotation of the powerful blades created a loud, rhythmical 'woom'. Captivated by the turbines' size and power, I simultaneously wanted to stand still underneath them in awe, and run a mile from them in case the blades fell off and crushed me.

I was far behind schedule when I rolled into Facinas for lunch shortly before 2pm, but my arrival marked a welcome return to tarmac. The most hazardous part of the day's journey was over.

It was a psychological boost to be back on a road and I intended to make the most of it by rapidly clocking up the miles towards Tarifa. But I'd overlooked the clue provided by the turbines and hadn't accounted for the region's strong sea breeze. As I turned towards the coast, a punishing crosswind hindered my progress. Toiling under the ferocity of the sun, I focused my efforts on driving my thighs down to turn the pedals and keep the wheels moving forwards. The bike tottered as the wind tore through the gaps between my spokes and I stared jealousy at the passing cars that disappeared effortlessly into the distance.

Just north of Tarifa I was forced to get off my bike again and walk as the hills, moderate though they were, became too steep to conquer in top gear. My self-esteem took a knock as two people cycled past. Fortunately, I was alone and free from embarrassment for the most part as the rural road cut through the sun-scorched fields of yellow grassland. This isolation ended abruptly when I hit the main road to Tarifa.

All at once, I was back among heavy traffic, alongside cars with surfboards attached to their roofs. The road ran parallel to the sweeping Los Lances beach, but squeezed in as I was to the hard shoulder, I wasn't tempted to hang about. As soon as I reached the outskirts of Tarifa I stopped and entered the first hostel I came across. It was full of restless surfers with long blonde hair whose wave chasing ambitions had been thwarted by the bemusingly calm sea.

I was told I'd need to wait an hour to check in, so I left my bag in reception and walked across the road to the beach. Curiously, I had the blindingly white expanse of sand almost all to myself. It reminded me of mythical Zihuatanejo Beach, where Morgan Freeman's Red meets Tim Robbins' Andy Dufresne at the end of *Shawshank Redemption*.

It quickly became apparent why I didn't have company. The wind was relentless.

The unique conditions generated by the Strait of

Gibraltar have led Tarifa to become the European capital for windsurfers and kitesurfers. The narrow strip of sea creates a powerful funnel effect when either the *Levante* (the easterly wind from Africa) or *Poniente* (the westerly wind from the Atlantic Ocean) is blowing. That day it was the former and the blustery wind had deterred everyone from staying on the shore for long. Even on the water, only a couple of resolute kitesurfers could be seen dancing on the surface.

The tide was out and the deep blue sea was a couple of hundred metres in front of me. Normally I'd have made a beeline for it, but I knew the Atlantic Ocean would be bracingly cold in comparison to the sheltered waters of the Mediterranean that I had enjoyed in recent weeks. Instead, I lazily kicked off my trainers, allowing my feet to sink into the deep, fine sand before collapsing happily on the spot. It was strange to see the sea so flat while the wind buffeted me with constant reminders of its potency. I had to admit that while I'd been looking forward to going surfing, I was too tired to have caught many waves and I was grateful the wind conditions had saved me from myself.

Keeping my mouth closed to keep out the sand blowing all around me, I closed my eyes briefly to let my achievement sink in. I had made it all the way to the very bottom of Spain, a place so far south, the African capital cities of Tunis and Algiers were further north than I now was. It felt fantastic. When I opened my eyes again moments later, my shoes had all but disappeared under a mountain of sand.

After a short call home, I emptied my shoes of the bucketloads of sand that had accumulated and returned to the hostel. I claimed a vacant bed (top bunk of course) by throwing my stuff on it, and set off to explore the city centre. I'd anticipated that the fame of its southerly location may outweigh the interest of the place itself, but Tarifa is far from a forgotten backwater. The city is surprisingly large and cosmopolitan, with a palpably different feel to that of other Andalusian cities. Populated by surfers who came and never left, it oozes an easygoing, bohemian vibe, characterised by shabby-chic coffee bars and tattoo parlours.

Tarifa's old town is inside Puerta de Jerez, the only remaining gate through the old Moorish city walls. Passing through it, I reached the central square which, confusingly, has three names: Plaza de Santa Maria (its official name), Plaza Alfonso XIII (its former name) and Plaza de la Ranita (its colloquial name). Ranita is a reference to the star-shaped water fountain in the plaza which is adorned with eight small ceramic frogs. It's one of many examples of the Moroccan influence on the city.

At the far end of town is the Castle of Tarifa, known locally as Castillo de Guzmán el Bueno. Built in the 10th century, it takes its name from Perez de Guzman, the commander tasked with defending the city from a Moorish siege in 1294. In an attempt to force de Guzmán's hand, the attackers captured his son and informed him that he would be killed if the population of Tarifa did not surrender. De Guzmán refused to countenance such an idea and, in a show of defiance, reportedly threw down his knife to the invaders for them to carry out their threat. They did so, but failed to seize control of Tarifa.

From the castle I could clearly make out, not only the

Rif mountains across the strait, but startlingly, the shapes of some of the buildings on Morocco's coastline. Where I was standing, only 14km separate Europe and Africa. It's easy to see why so many people risk their lives every year in search of a better life in a land they can see, but are prohibited from putting down roots in.

A stone's throw from the castle is the causeway, which stretches several hundred metres to the Island of Doves. Built at the start of the 19th century, it separates the Atlantic Ocean on one side and the Mediterranean on the other. It sounds idyllic, but in reality it is frequently anything but. By the time I got there, the sky had clouded over and the strong off-shore wind made it difficult to walk in a straight line. Armed with local knowledge, Tarifa's residents were wrapped up against the cold in thick winter coats as they walked their dogs. In comparison, the polyester jumper I had bought in Benidorm was now not only ugly, but woefully inadequate. At the end of the causeway, an imposing steel gate and a government sign instructed sightseers to turn back. It is only in the last two decades that the Island of Doves has ceased to be used as a military outpost. Since then, it has served as a temporary holding point for illegal immigrants.

I returned to the mainland in search of dinner. As I'd criss-crossed my way through Tarifa I had been on the lookout for bike shops to repair, or most likely replace, my derailleur. The couple of expensive looking stores I found were, predictably, closed on a Sunday. Worse still, they adopted a typically laid-back attitude to the start of the working week and didn't open until noon the next day.

I had already booked my accommodation on the Spanish border with Gibraltar for the following night and I'd promised myself I would be there in time to watch England's first match of the World Cup. I had long imagined how sweet the beer would taste as the game kicked off.

It was foolish to try to reach the border at La Línea de la Concepción without expecting the bike to have more problems, but I began to think that now it had made it this far, perhaps it could get me to Algeciras. The city was more than 20km away, but I knew I'd be able to find a cheap place to patch up my bike there so that I could make it to Gibraltar without further drama.

29

Tarifa to La Línea de la Concepción

I was up early for the final cycle of the trip. No one else was around at breakfast so I ate as much as I could from the cereal boxes laid out on the kitchen table in the hostel and departed with an apple in my pocket for lunch. On the map it looked like there was a path through Estrecho Natural Park to Algeciras, but when I asked at the hostel reception about the feasibility of cycling along the route I was told, definitively, the terrain was unrideable.

Reluctantly, I heeded the advice and joined the main road heading east. I'd hoped to avoid the traffic by starting early, but I got caught up in a convoy of articulated lorries spewing pollution in my face as I walked along the hard shoulder of the arduous climb. The only saving grace was that near the top was the Mirador del Estrecho. A vantage point of international renown, it provides spectacular views across to Africa. Standing tall across the strait is Morocco's 851-metre peak Jebel Musa, which is considered to be one of the Pillars of Hercules.

From the viewpoint, the road began its descent towards Algeciras. Free-wheeling down the hill, it no longer mattered that I was stuck in the highest gear and it was liberating to feel the rush of the air on my face again. The long-awaited sight of the Rock of Gibraltar - the other Pillar of Hercules - didn't disappoint. The brief glimpse of the finish line sparked a concoction of emotions so visceral that they threatened to get the better of me. I still had some way to go though and the heavy traffic approaching Algeciras was a deflating reminder of the pressing need to refocus my attention on the task in hand.

Few tourists come to Algeciras, and many of those that do quickly board the ferry to Morocco. Online travel forums dedicated to the city are littered with questions regarding personal safety and it's true that, as one of the world's biggest ports, the area is a hotspot for crime and a lucrative stomping ground for drug smugglers.

Following a brief stop in the admittedly perfectly pleasant María Cristina Park, I too was off, negotiating a complex web of roads to reach a bike shop in an out-of-town retail park. This close to the end of the journey, I was tempted not to repair the bike and hope it carried me to the peninsula. However, I had already advertised the bike online with the description 'in good condition with a few scratches'. If this was a little generous at the time, it wasn't even close to being an accurate representation anymore. I knew that even if I offered a heavy discount, the prospective buyer would almost certainly walk away, so I splashed the cash to repair the bike and kept my fingers crossed that the buyer would hold up their end of the bargain.

When the bike was fixed, it felt like I had a new lease of life. I changed gears for fun as I cycled around the Bay of Gibraltar. After so much spectacular scenery over the preceding weeks, the final section was inevitably a little underwhelming. I cycled past anonymous industrial plants before the traffic gradually built up along the rubbish-strewn, pot-holed roads on the outskirts of the town of La Línea de la Concepción. Finding an affordable place to stay in Gibraltar had proved impossible, so I'd booked accommodation on the Spanish side of the border, with the intention of completing the last leg of the journey on foot the next day.

As a consequence of its location, La Línea de la Concepción has always been associated with smuggling. While penicillin, sugar and coffee were the original contraband, in the 1980s and 1990s smugglers focused their efforts on trafficking cheap tobacco from Gibraltar into Spain. When authorities cracked down on this, smugglers diversified into the cannabis extract hashish. Their numbers swelled in the aftermath of the 2008 economic crisis, when many unemployed construction workers sought alternative means to pay their bills.

Unemployment in the town stands at around 35% and in the worst affected barrios, up to 80% of young people are out of work. Disturbingly, 3,000 of La Línea de la

Concepción's 64,000 residents are believed to be involved in the 30 or so gangs importing drugs from Morocco. According to the UN's 2017 World Drug Report, the African country was the world's biggest producer of hashish that year.

The barely concealed underbelly of Algeciras and La Línea de la Concepción has contributed to the province of Cadiz becoming 'the entry point for the greatest quantity of illegal drugs in the whole of the EU' according to Francisco Mena, chairman of the regional anti-drugs association. The year before, authorities had confiscated 145 tonnes of hashish and nearly 12 tonnes of cocaine in the region, yet Mena estimated 'only between 10% to 15% of the drugs smuggled through here are seized by the authorities'. The situation was threatening to boil over in the weeks prior to my arrival. More than 20 alleged drug smugglers had recently stormed the local hospital to extract an injured trafficker from custody and in an interview with *The Guardian* the town's mayor, Juan Franco, admitted regretfully that 'People expect there to be shootouts here.'

I approached the address of my accommodation, but I wasn't yet ready to stop. Over the past few weeks I had developed an almost daily routine. Each morning I packed my few possessions and set off to see what was around the corner. All I had to do was keep pedalling. It was hard, but it was simple. Going back home would involve finding a place to live, finding a job and returning to the mundane complexities of daily life. I pushed such thoughts to the back of my mind and purposefully cycled past where I was staying until I hit the sea.

Facing south, the arresting sight of the Rock of

Gibraltar dominated the skyline. I stood proudly in front of it and asked a middle-aged woman standing nearby to take my photograph. I was tempted to replicate the celebration of thousands of long-distance cyclists before me and hold my bike up above my head, but I knew the frame and the accompanying pannier bags were far too heavy to lift. Or, in light of the debacle removing my wheel in Alcalá de los Gazules, maybe I was just too weak. Regardless, the sense of achievement of reaching this point was profound and I was unable to resist explaining the significance of the photo to the woman.

She couldn't have been less interested. Eager to share my news with someone who cared, I called Sarah and happily told her I'd be coming home soon.

Almost as importantly, I had arrived in plenty of time to watch the football.

I dragged myself away from the beach and went to drop my stuff off. I had broken one of the cardinal rules of the trip and booked to stay my final couple of nights in the same property before I had seen it in person. What could go wrong?

Entry to the accommodation was via self check-in, so I picked up the keys and walked into the block of flats. Inside the property itself, the walls around the single bed prevented me from closing the door if I put my bag on the floor, which made the space feel more like a cot than a room. I left my bag and my phone on the bed and went out to collect the rest of my gear from the pannier rack.

As I left the flat, the door slammed shut behind me and I had the horrible realisation that I'd left the keys inside. After uttering some obscenities, I evaluated my options. My bike wasn't locked so if I left the building I would have to take it with me. If I left the building, I wouldn't be able to get back in. Even if I managed to borrow a phone to call my Airbnb host, he might be hundreds of kilometres away and unable to help. Hesitantly, I knocked on a neighbour's door on the off-chance they had a spare key. Fortuitously, not only were they in, but they did indeed have a spare set. Once I'd assured them I wasn't a burglar conducting an elaborate heist, they handed me the key.

The property listing had specified that bikes couldn't be left in the flat. Not that there was any space to do so. But, having spent £50 on my bike just hours earlier, I didn't want to leave it in the street and risk it being stolen the night before I hoped to sell it. So I locked it up, out of anyone's way, against the metal railings on the landing outside the flat. I hoped this would be ok and accepted I might need to move it if asked. Double-checking I had my keys and phone this time, I went back to the beach.

I sat happily on the sand, running through the highlights of the journey in my mind. When I checked my phone a little later, I had two missed calls from an unknown number. While I couldn't comprehend all of the Spanish in the voicemails, it was evident the caller was not happy. Once I had listened to each of the messages three times, I worked out it was my absent landlord demanding I move my bike. He sounded disproportionately agitated, so I hurriedly walked back to the flat and reluctantly locked my bike outside.

When I returned to the flat to grab a snack, I was met by a very angry man in the kitchen. He didn't say hello or introduce himself, so at first I hoped he might just be a fellow lodger. It soon became clear this wasn't the case.

'*¿Por qué dejaste tu bicicleta en el piso? En el anuncio indica que no se debería hacer eso,*' he demanded. Why did you leave your bike in the flat? The online listing asks you not to.

'*Lo siento.*' I'm sorry, I said, trying to placate him. Diffusing this unexpectedly tense situation was going to be a test of my Spanish. '*Pensé que si dejaba mi bicicleta fuera del piso en el pasillo estaría bien. Me dijo que no lo era y lo moví inmediatamente. No occurirá otra vez.*' I thought if I left my bike in the corridor outside the flat it was ok. When you told me it wasn't, I moved it immediately. It will not happen again.

The fraught nature of the conversation was affecting my fluency, and my uncertainty over whether to use the preterite or imperfect tense wasn't helping. All I wanted was to celebrate my arrival, and a confrontation with my landlord really wasn't how I wanted to spend my time.

'*Rompiste las reglas y no puedo confiar en ti. Debes irte mañana,*' the landlord replied. You broke the rules and I cannot trust you. You must leave tomorrow.

'*¿Que? ¿En serio?*' What? Are you serious?

For all my genuine incredulity at the escalating circumstances, I was pleased to have the opportunity to use in anger one of my favourite Spanish phrases, *¿En serio?*, with the customary accompanying raised eyebrow. '*La bicicleta estaba solo en el pasillo durante casi 45 minutos. No entiendo por qué no tienes confianza: moví la bicicleta cuando querías.*' The bike was alone in the hall for almost 45 minutes. I do not understand why you don't have trust - I moved the bike when you wanted. My Spanish was at breaking point, but grammatical nuance was fast becoming irrelevant.

The landlord moved forward a step, squaring up to me as he said, '*Quiero que te vayas ahora. Recoge tus maletas y vete.*' I want you to leave now. Take your bags and get out.

The situation was threatening to boil over into more than a verbal disagreement. My host was smaller than me, but his irrational behaviour meant I couldn't rule out the possibility he might suddenly pull out a kitchen knife from the drawer next to him. I could feel myself reddening as I gauged how best to react. I had no desire to stay with someone with such psychopathic tendencies, and I didn't want to give him my business either. But equally, I had nowhere else to go. It seemed unlikely I would be able to find, book and relocate to another Airbnb accommodation in the same price bracket within the next few hours.

'*Lo siento,*' I said, pathetically prioritising my desire to watch the football over my principles.

'*Bueno. Ahora vete.*' Good. Now get out.

I could feel a burning flash of red anger deep within me and my whole body tensed. I had travelled across Spain and at the finish line, I had the misfortune to meet this piece of work. It crossed my mind that I was making this too personal. Maybe he regularly used flimsy pretences to evict guests and keep their money. I felt completely impotent. If this was the way it was to go, I wanted to at least leave him with some food for thought.

'*Voy a llamar a Airbnb y les diré sobre ti.*' I'm going to call Airbnb and tell them about you. I wasn't above telling tales. I also wasn't going to waste any more brain power using the formal Spanish 'you' on an individual I no longer had a shred of respect for.

'*Hazlo*,' he said coolly. '*Ya he hablado con ellos.*' Do it. I've already spoken to them.

At that moment there were a million things I wanted to say to him and they haunted me all the way back to England. But I wanted to make sure he didn't kick me out before I had the chance to collect my stuff. He watched me closely as I hurriedly gathered my belongings and walked towards the entrance to the block of flats.

Out of his reach, I turned round like a petulant child and said very slowly and deliberately, '*Eres muy, muy estúpido y eres no muy simpático.*' You are very, very stupid and you are not very kind. I knew such insults would hardly cause him to lose any sleep, so I made one last aside that might. '*Disfruta tu revisión.*' Enjoy your review.

I called Airbnb to explain the situation straight away. To their credit, they were helpful. They had indeed received a call from my incandescent host approximately 30 minutes earlier. He had been told that if he felt sufficiently aggrieved he could ask me to leave the following morning, but that under no circumstances could he kick me out onto the street. To resolve the situation, the call handler began contacting alternative nearby hosts and just over an hour later I had a place to stay. It was significantly more expensive, but Airbnb agreed to pay the difference by transferring the money onto my account. This process was complicated by the fact that my card had been blocked ever since I'd arrived in Marbella, when my bank noticed 'I' had inexplicably purchased four fridges in Istanbul that afternoon.

While going through Airbnb's security checks, I walked restlessly back and forth along the promenade.

Thankfully I was unaware I was just 400 metres away from Calle Canarias, a street reputed to be one of the most dangerous in Europe. By the time my new accommodation was confirmed, there was only 10 minutes until England began their World Cup campaign against Tunisia. I had assumed La Línea de la Concepción's relative proximity to both Gibraltar and Tunisia would mean it would be easy to find a place to watch the game. Once again, I was wrong.

I dashed from one bar to the next until I at last found a small television showing the match in an empty fish restaurant. The owner was unmistakably ambivalent about the result, but chuckled to himself as he watched me become increasingly vexed by England's underwhelming performance. After an injury time winner ensured England made a winning start to the tournament, I set off into the gathering gloom to find my new lodgings across the other side of town.

I was met by a portly, unshaven Greek called Angelo. He was in his sixties and had a strong cockney accent on account of the many years he had lived in London. I warmed to him instantly. He gave me a key, but told me I wouldn't need it for he never locked the door.

'Are you not worried about security?' I asked.

'No,' he said, waving his arms around the sheets of paper haphazardly scattered across his poorly lit living room. 'There's nothing here of value for anyone to steal anyway. Besides I know everyone around here.' I wasn't sure whether this last statement was a show of faith in the upstanding community of La Línea de la Concepción, or a subtle hint that anyone who crossed him would live to regret it.

Angelo lived alone. He spoke endearingly of an ex-wife he had left behind in England many years before in such a way that suggested he couldn't bear to be with her - or without her. His large house was fitted with wood panelling interiors that hadn't been touched since the 1960s. Neither, it seemed, had the electrical wiring, as the floors were covered in a web of extension leads all connecting back to the one socket in the house that worked.

I didn't mind at all - I was simply relieved to have a bed. (And that England had won.)

30

Gibraltar

The next morning I walked along the coast for 40 minutes to reach the border. I had previously visited Gibraltar in 2005, when, in surreal circumstances, I had received my GCSE results atop of the Rock from that year's Miss Gibraltar. This provided ample distraction from the fact that I'd failed to deliver in the subjects I liked most: English and History. Perhaps I'll send a copy of this book to my respective teachers to let them know their efforts weren't in vain.

In hindsight, I was born four years too early. The Miss Gibraltar of 2009 was later crowned Miss World. Taking into account Gibraltar's population size - equivalent to that of a small town - it was a remarkable achievement and jubilant street parades were held in her honour. At the time of my cycle, the former Miss World was mayor of Gibraltar. Who said you can't have beauty and brains?

As I'd been to Gibraltar before I decided not to return to the summit of the Rock, and thus avoided the tribes of barbary macaques that live there, preying on dim-witted tourists. Instead, I intended to find out what else the British Overseas Territory had to offer.

Considering the Gibraltarian border is located next to a major drug trafficking hotspot, and its very existence is controversial, you might expect passengers to be subject to stringent security measures. But the bag checking scanners sat idle as we were waved through with only the slightest glance at our identification. After passing through customs, I walked along the main road which intersects the runway. Others were doing likewise, but it nevertheless felt disconcerting as the route was delineated solely by a few dashes of white paint.

The existence of this thoroughfare, which temporarily closes every time a plane is due to land, is one of the reasons why Gibraltar Airport is deemed to be the most dangerous in Europe. Pilots are wary of the strong crosswinds that swirl around the Rock, while beachgoers are astonished by how close the planes fly over their heads as they come in to land. In spite of the challenges posed by the runway's location, it's noteworthy that no one has been hurt in an accident since World War II, when the prime minister of the Polish government in exile, Władysław Sikorski, was one of 16 people who died when their plane crashed into the sea seconds after take-off. Many believe even this crash wasn't a consequence of poor conditions or pilot error, and are convinced the plane was sabotaged.

As with other remnants of the British Empire, Gibraltar is a geo-political oddity. I remember as a child struggling to understand how Britain, my honourable homeland, could continue to exercise its claim to a landmass nearly 2,000km away from the white cliffs of Dover. And if Britain's geographic connection to Gibraltar seems tenuous, so too are its historical ties.

When Charles II of Spain died childless in 1700 having chosen his grandnephew Philip as his successor, Philip's ascension was directly opposed by several other major European nations on the grounds that he was already heir to the throne in France. Britain, Austria and the Netherlands refused to countenance a potential union between Spain and France, so the three countries came together to form the Grand Alliance to ensure their preferred candidate, Archduke Charles of Austria, sat on the Spanish throne.

Capturing Gibraltar was part of this effort, but the Spanish population weren't receptive to the idea and fled inland. After a decade of fierce fighting, the wisdom of the Grand Alliance's choice was under severe scrutiny when Charles' elder brother, Joseph, promptly died of smallpox, making Charles heir to the Austrian throne. Faced with the prospect of an alternative unwanted union, an end to the conflict was sought and the Treaty of Utrecht was signed in 1713. This permitted Philip to remain King of Spain on a number of conditions, among them his renunciation of his right to rule France and the ceding of Gibraltar to Britain. Just because.

In spite, or perhaps because, of the dubious grounds on which Britain claims Gibraltar, its population is fiercely patriotic. The 1967 referendum on Gibraltar's sovereignty showed that 99% of voters wanted Gibraltar to stay British. At the turn of the Millennium, the British government floated the idea of allowing Spain to have dual ownership of the territory, prompting Gibraltar to hold another referendum in protest. This produced the same result as 35 years before. The populous was pragmatic enough to acknowledge the importance of maintaining a cordial relationship with Spain when it came to Brexit though. Its 96% vote in support of remaining in the European Union was the highest of any electorate.

Gibraltar's unabashed patriotism makes it one of the few places where people openly celebrate their Britishness. I hadn't seen so many Union Jacks since the London Olympics. The tourist shop by the runway was packed to the rafters with naff cuddly red phone booths and masks of the royal family. Elsewhere, statues of British heroes such as Lord Nelson and Admiral George Rooke, who served as commander of the Grand Alliance fleet, are spread across the peninsula. Street names are also laden with civic pride, with the road across the runway named Winston Churchill Avenue.

There is a legend that when the macaques leave the Rock, so too will the British. When Churchill heard there were only seven macaques left on Gibraltar during World War II, he hastily ordered five females to be introduced from north Africa. I assumed this story was apocryphal, but government files reveal Churchill's consternation and his desire to ensure the number of macaques would never again fall below 24. Seeing as they currently number more than 230, it would appear Gibraltar will be remaining British for some time to come.

***

Maybe it was the fact we were all heading in the same direction, or that the crowd consisted largely of well-oiled, boisterous Brits, but the journey from the runway to the town centre resembled the walk to a football stadium on matchday. I may, as a consequence of my birth, technically have been supporting the same team, but looking dispassionately at the noisy horde descending on the town square, I couldn't blame the Spaniards for fleeing at the start of the 18th century.

The Grand Alliance's fears of a union between Spain and France materialised in the decades following the Treaty of Utrecht. Spain had retained its desire to regain control of Gibraltar and enlisted France's assistance to besiege the territory in 1779. One of the longest sieges in history ensued. The reason it lasted so long, and ultimately ended in failure, was because British ships carrying fresh supplies were consistently able to bypass the ineffectual blockade.

The frustrated Franco-Spanish forces gathered to launch an all-out attack. They outnumbered the British defensive forces by nine to one, yet suffered a humiliating defeat. This was in part thanks to the timely invention of the Koehler Depressing Carriage, a cannon built on a tilt, enabling it to be fired at steep downward-facing angles from the Rock of Gibraltar. One of these cannons now sits alongside the bars in Gibraltar's main plaza, Grand Casemates Square.

Although France and Spain had failed to conquer Gibraltar during the three years and seven months of the siege, their attacks left the town in ruins. Colonel John Drinkwater wrote at the time that the buildings 'exhibited a most dreadful picture of the effects of so animated a bombardment...in general the floors and roofs were destroyed, and the bare shell only was left standing'. The removal of some of this debris created space for a barracks at Grand Casemates Square, which also became the de facto site for public hangings.

Due south of the square is the pedestrianised Main Street. Walking along it, between outlets of British retailers such as Debenhams and Dorothy Perkins, it felt like a typical English high street. Having been forced to spend what felt like several lifetimes in such shops as a child, I was immune to their attractions and carried on towards the botanical gardens. At the entrance, I sidestepped the queue to ride the cable car to the top of the Rock and instead enjoyed the peaceful tranquility of the rest of the park. No one else was around, and it appeared the rowdy countrymen that I had crossed the border alongside hadn't made it past the Irish pubs and other home comforts.

As I was looking up at the trees above the intersecting garden paths, I felt something reptilian brush the bare skin of my sandalled feet. When I looked down, I saw a one-and-a-half-metre long snake slithering behind me into the bushes. I let out an involuntary squeal as a shiver of horror ran down my spine. Upon hearing this undignified, almost bestial noise, a man in his twenties wearing a smart green polo shirt, appeared behind a bush in front of me.

'Are you ok?' he asked.

'Yes,' I said, trying to regain my composure. 'A big snake just rubbed up against my foot.'

His face fell. Without saying a word, he vanished and started shouting urgently. 'Vanessa! Vanessa! Did you definitely shut the door...?'

At once, other people in similar green polo shirts started to emerge from all corners of the park. Most ran in the same direction he had, but the last to arrive asked me what the commotion was. I noticed a crest on his shirt bore the words 'Alameda Wildlife Park'. I was telling him about the snake when the man who had first spoken to me returned.

'Phew, ok, panic over. Sorry about that. We've just had feeding time for the snakes and I was worried the python had escaped. You had me worried.'

'How big is it?' I asked.

'It's a three-metre long albino Burmese Python. He's called Duke.'

I laughed - I didn't think I wanted to be on first name terms with Duke.

'So what did I see?' I was curious to understand why he was so unconcerned by the fact that there was still a large snake on the loose.

'It was probably a horseshoe whip snake,' he said, not giving much thought to the question.

'It was yellow with large brown circles,' I persisted, hoping these details would reignite his interest.

'Yeah, they are the ones.'

'Are they poisonous?'

'No,' he replied, amused by the predictable nature of my questions.

Disappointed by his answers, I walked away to find

out more online about the dangers posed by horseshoe whip snakes. The complete lack of threat the snake represented was illustrated by the fact that the search results yielded information not about the dangers the snake posed to me, but the perils it faces from humans. These include fast moving traffic and snake charmers.

It hadn't quite been life or death, but I decided any further excitement on British soil could wait until I returned home. I headed back across the border to my accommodation, where I washed my bike in preparation for selling it that evening. I was keen for everything to go smoothly as I'd had a traumatic experience in similar circumstances in London a couple of years before. I had tried to buy a bike listed on Gumtree and when I arrived, the 'sellers', incorrectly assuming I was carrying a large wad of cash (I wasn't born yesterday), tried to rob me. I ran as fast as I could to safety and called the police. When they picked me up, they told me someone else a few weeks before had been snared in a similar way nearby and, unable to evade their attackers, had been fatally stabbed.

This time, if things went well, I would end up having an extra €100 in my pocket - and the buyer would know it. I had fatalistic visions of selling the bike, only for the buyer to rob me of the money and then ride off into the sunset on my bike. Even if I wasn't dealing with a criminal, I knew the seller may simply not turn up, or decide the bike wasn't for him, leaving me with only hours to sell it before my flight home.

We agreed to meet in Plaza de la Constitución, a large public square in La Línea de la Concepción at 7pm. Treating it like an international hostage swap, I arrived early and sat on a park bench with my back to the wall, so that I could see the buyer approach. I wasn't going to be ambushed again. A few minutes past the hour, a rotund man strolled up towards me.

'Are you Chris?'

In normal circumstances this would have been a good opportunity to practise my Spanish. However, I decided I wouldn't insist on using the native tongue, for if I was to be mugged, I at least wanted to know what was happening.

'Yes,' I replied, hoping my smile masked my inner turmoil.

I had to admit the man didn't look like he was about to mug me. He was a few years older than me, a couple of inches smaller and dressed in a baggy black T-shirt, shorts and flip-flops. Given this, I was confident I could outrun him if necessary and relaxed accordingly as I began my sales patter.

The man didn't need much persuading and, after giving the bicycle a brief test ride while I watched on nervously, he handed me the money and departed with the bike. Still feeling ill at ease, I walked briskly away from the scene of the transaction and turned down a succession of side streets at random in order to lose anyone in case I was being followed. Of course, no one was on my tail. When I had reassured myself I was safe, I sat down in a small square filled with cafes.

I instantly broke down into tears.

My reaction caught me completely by surprise and I sobbed uncontrollably. As a result of the frightening incident in London, I'd looked forward to getting the transaction over with. I was in need of the money and I no longer required the bike. But I was also now, definitively, at the end of my journey. There could be no more cycling. The bike which I had so callously traded away had enabled me to push my limits and allowed me to enjoy and endure experiences that would otherwise have been out of reach.

It had tried and tested me, but my frustrations were never aimed at the bike. How could they be? This was a bike designed, according to the retailer, 'for riding on flat or slightly undulated terrain' with 'short-distance moderate pace commuters' in mind. No, the frustrations I'd felt were only at my own incompetence. My humble bicycle had surpassed every realistic expectation a customer could have. And while it may have broken down on occasion, its struggles only matched my own.

As my sole companion over the previous month and a half, I had come to love the bike with a passion that defied logic. Now I would never see it again. Rubbing the tears from my eyes, I realised people seated under the cafe awnings were looking at me. The last thing I wanted was a well-meaning individual to check if I was ok and for me to have to explain in snivelling Spanish the cause of my distress. So I composed myself and went looking for a world-renowned remedy to ameliorate my mood and dry my tears: a great, big ice cream.

I meandered back towards my accommodation and grabbed a last supper at Mercadona. Feeling flush with cash, I bought the final muffin of the trip and upgraded the customary banana in my sandwich to cheese. Looking south towards the Rock, I ate dinner on the shore and watched the sand trickle through my fingers as I wondered when I would next be on a beach. Filled with melancholy, I got up and continued walking around the Bay of Gibraltar. The light slowly disappeared from the sky until all I could see of the peninsula were the lights of the airport.

I gently pushed open the door of Angelo's house to find him and another man halfway through what appeared to be a heavy drinking session. Two tumblers sat on the coffee table next to an open bottle of whiskey. Angelo was sitting in an armchair while the other man lay across the adjacent sofa. He was balding and had only the two middle buttons of his shirt done up, revealing a hairy chest, and rather more prominently, a pot belly.

'Oi, oi you wanker!' he proclaimed cheerfully in my direction.

'John, please, he is my guest!' It was clear Angelo was not, thankfully, quite as far gone as his friend.

'What? It's fine: he's a wanker, I'm a wanker, we're all wankers. Isn't that right?' John looked in my direction, waiting for me to confirm that I was, as he had adjudged from the moment he saw me, a wanker.

I wasn't sure how to respond. Normally I'd have happily entered into some lighthearted verbal jousting, but I just wasn't in the mood.

Perhaps it wasn't so bad to be leaving after all. A new chapter awaited me in England, where I would live with Sarah for the first time. Hopefully, she wouldn't call me a wanker every time I arrived home.

'I guess,' I answered at last, hoping that would appease John so I could head upstairs to start packing. 'Goodnight.'

Epilogue

Shortly after returning to England, I moved to Cambridge. Sarah is no longer my girlfriend, but my wife. Although Covid-19 delayed our nuptials not once, but twice, we got there in the end. Having spent a year away in South America and Spain, I settled back into normal life, with my daily ride restricted to the 6km commute into the office.

Occasionally, I see the same model of bike I used during my trip. Just as when I see a border terrier that has a passing resemblance to the family dog we had when I was a child, I always take a moment to appreciate it. The bike's utilitarian design means no one else would look twice, but the sight of its modest frame immediately transports me back to those glorious, carefree sunny days on the road in Spain.

About the Author

Since spending five years working in the television studios at Sky News and BT Sport in London, Chris has worked as a freelance writer and digital marketer.

Prior to setting off on his bike in Spain he lived in Panama for five months, managing the social media channels of the country's largest language school.

On his return to the UK he oversaw the digital marketing for an artificial intelligence start-up company in Cambridge and has written for numerous publications including The Times, The Huffington Post and Metro.

Find out more about Chris - and be among the first to learn of future book releases - by signing up to his newsletter at https://chrisatkinonline.com/newsletter/.

Acknowledgements

On so many levels I'm hugely grateful to Sarah for her unstinting support. Sarah not only understood my desire to explore Spain by bike, but also provided encouragement and excellent editorial advice at every stage of the writing process.

Thanks too to Richard Chatterton for tolerating my countless questions regarding the accuracy of the Spanish grammar used in the book. I'd also like to thank Jay Loe for the book cover and the map illustrating my journey across the country.

The book would of course be very different were it not for the diverse characters who allowed me into their homes during the trip. Several of them showed great kindness towards me, in particular Lucia who hosted me in Torrox-Costa at the end of a day that I will never forget.